BONSAI

The Complete and Comprehensive Guide for Beginners

By Kaito Tanaka

© Copyright 2019 - All rights reserved.

The content contained within this book may not be reproduced, duplicated or transmitted without direct written permission from the author or the publisher.

Under no circumstances will any blame or legal responsibility be held against the publisher, or author, for any damages, reparation, or monetary loss due to the information contained within this book. Either directly or indirectly.

Legal Notice:

This book is copyright protected. This book is only for personal use. You cannot amend, distribute, sell, use, quote or paraphrase any part, or the content within this book, without the consent of the author or publisher.

Disclaimer Notice:

Please note the information contained within this document is for educational and entertainment purposes only. All effort has been executed to present accurate, up to date, and reliable, complete information. No warranties of any kind are declared or implied. Readers acknowledge that the author is not engaging in the rendering of legal, financial, medical or professional advice. The content within this book has been derived from various sources.

Please consult a licensed professional before attempting any techniques outlined in this book.

By reading this document, the reader agrees that under no circumstances is the author responsible for any losses, direct or indirect, which are incurred as a result of the use of information contained within this document, including, but not limited to, — errors, omissions, or inaccuracies.

Table of Contents

INTRODUCTION VII
THE WONDERFUL BONSAI VII
CHAPTER 1 - WHAT IS BONSAI? 1
- THE DIFFERENT ASPECTS OF BONSAI PLANTS 4
- A SHORT HISTORY OF BONSAI 7
- INTERESTING FACTS ABOUT BONSAI 10

CHAPTER 2 - ALL ABOUT BONSAI PLANTS 15
- STYLES OF BONSAI PLANTS 16
- TYPES OF BONSAI PLANTS 22
- CHOOSING YOUR BONSAI 53

CHAPTER 3 - PREPARING TO GROW YOUR BONSAI 56
- GROWING A BONSAI FROM A SEED 57
- SELECTING A HEALTHY STARTER BONSAI 62
- CHOOSING THE PERFECT POT FOR YOUR BONSAI 64

CHAPTER 4 - GROWING BASICS 69
- BASIC TOOLS YOU NEED FOR GROWING YOUR BONSAI 70
- BASIC CARE TIPS FOR GROWING BONSAI 79
- STYLING AND SHAPING TECHNIQUES 82

CHAPTER 5 - PLANTING AND REPOTTING 89
- CHOOSING THE BEST SOIL FOR YOUR BONSAI 89
- TIPS FOR PLANTING 94

BONSAI

Tips for Repotting 96

CHAPTER 6 - PRUNING AND TRIMMING 101

How to Properly Prune Your Bonsai 104
Clever Trimming Techniques 110

CHAPTER 7 - WATERING AND FERTILIZING 114

Proper Ways of Watering Bonsai Plants 117
Do Bonsai Plants Need Fertilizer? 123

CHAPTER 8 - WIRING TECHNIQUES AND CLAMPING 128

Various Wiring Techniques to Try 131
What Does Clamping Mean in Bonsai Growing? 136

CHAPTER 9 - DEFOLIATION AND DEADWOOD TECHNIQUES 139

How to Defoliate Your Bonsai Plant 140
Deadwood Techniques for Bonsai 145

CHAPTER 10 - INDOOR AND OUTDOOR BONSAI 149

Differences Between Indoor and Outdoor Bonsai 150
Growing Indoor Bonsai 153
Growing Outdoor Bonsai 157

CHAPTER 11 - BONSAI SEASONAL CARE TIPS 163

Caring for Your Bonsai During Spring 165
Caring for Your Bonsai During Summer 167
Caring for Your Bonsai During Autumn 169
Caring for Your Bonsai During Winter 171

CHAPTER 12 - MISTAKES TO AVOID WHEN

BONSAI

GROWING BONSAI TREES 174
   BE AWARE OF AND AVOID THESE COMMON
   MISTAKES 175
CONCLUSION - PLANTING YOUR OWN BONSAI 178

INTRODUCTION

THE WONDERFUL BONSAI

Bonsai isn't just a plant. It's a form of art which is becoming more and more popular all across the world. Although growing bonsai is something people would love to start, many find the whole process intimidating. Before the internet became a permanent part of our lives, it was extremely difficult to obtain some great bonsai resources. But now, the issue is how to sort through all of the resources available online to find the best and most helpful information to help anyone interested in growing bonsai.

The good news is, this is where this book comes in.

From learning all about bonsai — what it means, its history, types, tips for choosing bonsai, and more — to some practical tips to help you start your own bonsai growing journey, this book will serve as your all-around resource. Bonsai isn't something new. In fact, it has a long history tracing back to about a thousand years. Bonsai is considered a form of "living art" involving taking ordinary trees then using small pots to grow them for the purpose of restricting their growth.

For any bonsai artist, their aim is to "create" trees which are artificially perfect and can resemble the huge ones that grow in nature. Often, people refer to bonsai growing as a hobby, but those who are actually doing it consider bonsai an art form. But unlike other forms of art, bonsai doesn't have an end — that is unless your bonsai dies. But if you care for your plant properly, you may be able to pass it on to your children and to the next generation for them to take care of.

Each bonsai is unique. Those who grow bonsai aren't limited by anything but their imagination, skills, and how much time and effort they put into improving the aesthetic appeal of their plants. However, these days, there are now classification systems which may be of help to bonsai growers to closely mimic the look and form of trees in nature. When it comes to bonsai, the size of the plant depends on the size of your chosen pot. Therefore, when you've made the decision to grow bonsai, this is one of the many aspects you will have to consider throughout the whole process.

BONSAI

Before you start growing bonsai, you should first learn all that you can about it, so you know exactly what you're getting yourself into. As a matter of fact, making the choice to grow bonsai is a lot like making the choice to bring a pet into your home. As simple as the task may seem for some, it does involve some level of commitment, especially if you want to grow a bonsai plant that will last for generations to come.

If you know what you're doing and you're careful with how you handle your plant, you can have your own bonsai in a matter of months. Then all you would have to do is keep on caring for your plant and maintain it to keep it healthy and flourishing. With that being said, let's begin your learning process.

BONSAI

CHAPTER 1

WHAT IS BONSAI?

The term "Bon-sai" is actually Japanese in origin and it literally translates to "planted in a container." It is a very popular art form that comes from an ancient horticultural practice in China. Later on, part of this practice was re-developed under the Zen Buddhists' influence in Japan. This practice has been in existence for more than a thousand years now and these days, more and more people are becoming interested in growing bonsai of their very own. It's important to note that bonsai aren't plants which have been genetically dwarfed. As a matter of fact, you can use virtually any species of trees to grow bonsai.

The art of growing bonsai involves techniques such as wiring, pruning, defoliation, and more, all of which we will be discussing in this book. It also involves the careful restriction—but not the abandonment—of fertilizers in order to promote the healthy growth of the plant. Most bonsai are only grown to a height of four feet and a lot of people find it easier to work with plant species that have smaller leaves, especially in terms of crafting the design.

To give you a more concrete idea of the types of plants you can use for growing bonsai, do this simple exercise:

Go outside and look at the plants in your garden. All of those hedges, bushes, trees, and even the plants in your nursery on in the wild can, essentially, be used as your starter material. Most types of native or local plant species can be grown as outdoor bonsai, while others can be grown indoors.

Ultimately, the main goal of growing bonsai is to create a miniature depiction of nature that is as realistic as possible. As your bonsai grows smaller, it will become increasingly abstract instead of mimicking nature in a more accurate way. There are several classifications of bonsai in existence. Although there is no "standard" size for these plants, knowing these classifications helps you get a better understanding of the botanical and aesthetic aspects of the plant. Originally, the basis of these classifications was the number of men it would take to lift the tree. Here are the most common classifications of bonsai according to size:

- Imperial which measures 60" to 80"

- Hachi-uye which measures 40" to 60"
- Omono or Dai which measures 30" to 48"
- Chumono or Chiu which measures 16" to 36"
- Katade-mochi which measures 10" to 18"
- Komono which measures 6" to 10"
- Shohin which measures 5" to 8"
- Mame which measures 2" to 6"
- Shito which measures 2" to 4"
- Keshitsubo which measures 1" to 3"

A bonsai tree is a miniature replication of nature which comes in the form of a tree. When done properly, it shouldn't show human intervention clearly. But there are other connotations to the meaning of the term "bonsai" which includes:

- A general style of shape that is tree-like.
- Relative smallness as compared with trees growing in nature.
- A sense of nature which has been accentuated by the intervention of human beings in a subtle way.
- A profile that isn't as authentic or detailed as

a tree but that has just the right number of features to suggest a tree.

- A transportable tree or portable oasis that represents the seasons and nature.
- Something of value that has received love and care for each day of its life in a container.

These are just some common ideas, but you can also come up with your own definition of what bonsai means to you.

The Different Aspects of Bonsai Plants

Although people have tried to define bonsai in different ways, there's no precise and clear statement anyone can use to really explain what bonsai means. The term does have a literal translation, but bonsai can mean different things to different people. This is especially true for those who have really studied bonsai, its history, the different types, how to care for bonsai, and so much more. As simple as this art form may seem to most people, it has various aspects which includes:

- Bonsai as a science and art

Bonsai is the science and art of shaping and dwarfing of a plant—usually a shrub or a tree—then growing it in a pot or some other kind of container. It's meant to depict a miniature plant in nature. These days though, several practitioners, authors, and masters have given bonsai a broader coverage.

Now, bonsai may include other types of plants that have hard stems, but they aren't botanically classified as trees or shrubs along with some types of herbaceous plants and grasses. Furthermore, bonsai may only consist of one plant, a pair of plants or a collection of them. The creation of bonsai is a complex process which involves a lot of steps such as choosing the proper soil and pot, planting, potting, repotting, trimming, wiring, and more.

Still, bonsai is first and foremost an art form. Any horticultural aspects of bonsai are considered secondary even though they are essential in the process of dwarfing as well as prolonging the tree's culture.

- Bonsai as a philosophy and religion

For a lot of cultures, the term bonsai and antiquity are synonymous. During ancient times, growing bonsai was a privilege in Japan and China; however, only a few people were able to do this art form. Furthermore, bonsai is commonly associated with philosophy and religion.

Originally, Buddhist monks who practiced bonsai during China's Han dynasty, was their way of communicating with God, the creator of nature and the universe. To them, they believed that being able to grow and cultivate was a way for them to show that they understood the idea of the world's creation. Moreover, they didn't produce bonsai from seeds, layering or cutting.

Instead, they searched for plants with a unique shape in the forests or mountains then cultivated it. Searching for such a plant had a symbolic meaning — it was considered a search for perfection in its truest form.

- Bonsai as an element of visual art

These days, bonsai is a recognized form of art as international and geographical competitions are periodically held for it. Bonsai possesses aesthetic elements including form, composition, proportion, line, balance, depth, and more. And these elements are similar to those of sculptures, paintings, and other visual art forms. The style and personality of those who grow bonsai can be easily recognized by experts.

Bonsai is considered both a dynamic form of art and a living sculpture. But unlike other art forms, bonsai never gets finished. If you don't properly care for your bonsai, several things may happen: the growth of the plant may speed up, it might grow into a different shape or it might wither away and die. But as other forms of art, you can analyze, teach, and learn bonsai.

- Bonsai as a challenge

Growing and cultivating bonsai isn't a simple task. You must learn all that you can about it in order to achieve success. Of course, putting in the time and effort will eventually give you the pleasure of this particular art form. As you see your bonsai grow, you will come to realize its true beauty and perfect harmony with the rest of nature.

Furthermore, the skills you need to succeed in bonsai growing don't come easily. It can take between a few months to a few years for you to be able to produce your own masterpiece which bears your own style and personality. But the moment you realize that you have grown something of such beauty, it will be in that moment when you'll also realize that all the time and effort you put into your bonsai was worth it. This feeling is a lot like the one felt by artists who create their art with painstaking precision. Yes, it's a challenge, but if you press on, you'll soon have your own unique piece of nature to appreciate and share with the rest of the world.

A Short History of Bonsai

Even though "bon-sai" is a Japanese term, the art form it describes actually originated in China. By 700

AD, Chinese people had already begun the art of bonsai which they referred to as "pun-sai" and which involved the use of special techniques to use containers to grow small trees. Since bonsai seems to have its roots in Japan and China, let's take a look at the history of bonsai in both countries.

The History of Bonsai in China

Around 5,000 years ago, bowls which have been flattened or shallow basins which were called "pun," "pan" or "pen" were used for growing bonsai in China. During the Bronze Age about one thousand years later, they had also used these containers for ceremonial purposes both political and religious in nature. Then around 1,200 years after that came the Chinese Five Agents Theory which involved the five elements: fire, metal, wood, earth, and water. With this theory came the development of the concept of growing miniature replicas.

For instance, when one recreates a mountain on a smaller scale, he or she may focus on the magical properties of the mountain then access these properties. The Chinese believed that the smaller the reproduction was compared to the original, the more powerful it was. The earliest trees which have been collected then grown in containers were twisted specimens with peculiar shapes from the wild. The Chinese considered these sacred because they couldn't be used for any ordinary purpose. They had grotesque forms that they believed symbolized long-life.

As centuries passed, various styles of these bonsai were developed throughout the country with its different landscapes. They used ceramic and earthenware containers to grow the trees which they displayed on stands made of wood. Then they tried to reshape the trees using lead strips, brass wire or frameworks made of bamboo. Writers and poets from the country made their own descriptions of these miniature trees, while painters included them as a representation of the lifestyle of cultivated men. By the 16th century, they referred to these miniature trees as "pun tsai" which means "tray planting." And by the 17th century, the term "Penjing" was used which means "tray landscape."

The History of Bonsai in China

According to the beliefs of the Japanese people, the very first "Penjing" or tray landscapes were brought to the country as religious souvenirs around 1,200 years ago. Two hundred years later, the very first written work of fiction in the country included a passage describing the religious souvenirs. However, it was only around 800 years ago that graphic portrayals of bonsai emerged in Japan as the Japanese were fascinated by all things Chinese.

Japanese Zen monks found beauty in these miniature trees, so they developed the tray landscapes further to allow a single tree to grow in a pot—and they made certain that this tree could represent much more than nature. Generally, the pots used by the Japanese were a lot deeper than the ones used in China. Back then, they called this form of gardening "hachi-no-ki" which literally translated to "the bowl's tree." Eventually, the art form had evolved into what the rest of the world now knows as bonsai which, as we've established, is now growing more and more in popularity.

Interesting Facts About Bonsai

Bonsai is an art form of planting and growing a tree

BONSAI

(or any other kind of plant) in a small container. Traditionally speaking, bonsai isn't grown for the purpose of medicine or food. Instead, the main purpose is to show the grower's discipline and hard work. For some, they grow bonsai to give them an opportunity to think and reflect on life. Before we go into the more technical information about bonsai, here are some fun facts you may find interesting:

- The origin of bonsai is in China

This may come as a surprise to a lot of people since bonsai is commonly considered a Japanese art form. But contrary to the belief of most people, bonsai started in China before gradually shifting to Japan. Later, the Japanese popularized this art form until it became a global phenomenon.

- You can grow bonsai from a seed

If you really want to get the full experience of growing bonsai, you may consider starting from a seed. For those who are really committed to the process, this is much more appealing than purchasing a fully-grown bonsai then maintaining it. Of course, growing bonsai from a seed is both time-consuming and challenging. But it is more rewarding in terms of the experience you will gain from the whole process. Just make sure that you purchase the bonsai seed from a reputable source and choose the seed(s) carefully.

- There are specific kinds of tools and equipment needed for growing bonsai

Growing bonsai is a specialized process; therefore, you may also have to purchase specialized kinds of tools and equipment to cultivate and maintain your plant. This is especially important when it comes to shaping and styling techniques to give your bonsai more personality and to make it truly one-of-a-kind. Later on, we will be going through these tools and equipment which you must purchase before you can start growing your bonsai.

- Buying fully-grown bonsai is more common for beginners

For those who would like to have their own bonsai, but don't think that they can grow one successfully, they have the option to purchase a plant that is already fully-grown. For such a case, you should purchase your plant from specialist bonsai growers to ensure that you're getting the best one for yourself. Do research on which shops offer fully-grown bonsai in your locale before you make a final choice.

- Many people consider bonsai as an investment

Whether you plan to grow bonsai from seed or maintain a fully-grown one, you need to invest a lot of time and care into it. Think of your bonsai as an investment and the more you put into it, the more rewarding it becomes. If you're one who wants quick results, then you may want to find a different hobby.

- Bonsai growing isn't just about gardening

Although being able to successfully grow a bonsai demonstrates your gardening skills, that's not the only thing it shows. Having a fully-grown bonsai also shows off your patience, stamina, and how well you're able to concentrate and commit to one thing. This is why some people also consider bonsai growing as an exercise in self-discipline. In fact, the traditional culture of Japan and China views bonsai growing as a test of the limit of one's acceptance and patience.

- Repotting bonsai isn't a one-time thing

As you will later on discover, it's vital to continue repotting your bonsai as it grows in vigor and size. As you see your bonsai flourish, you should re-pot it as needed. Changing your bonsai's pot is also important for its overall health and growth. Without this step, you might be hindering your bonsai from reaching its true potential.

- The style of bonsai you choose reflects your own personality

Remember that growing bonsai is a commitment.

Therefore, when choosing the style of your plant, make sure that it reflects your own personality. That way, as you see your bonsai grow and flourish, it will serve as your inspiration. Also, the style of the bonsai you choose must fit your lifestyle so you can care for it in the best possible way.

CHAPTER 2

ALL ABOUT BONSAI PLANTS

There's just something about these small trees that makes them so appealing to a lot of people. Bonsai has a unique character and a distinct presence that any other type of plant cannot provide. But as we've established—growing a bonsai isn't a simple or easy task. Often, people purchase their first bonsai trees but get disappointed when after a couple of months, their bonsai withers and dies. Unfortunately, some bonsai sellers aren't totally honest about the plants they sell. Often, those who buy the plants don't even know the name of the tree species nor do they know the health of the bonsai when they purchased in. In such cases, both the bonsai and the buyer would have been victims of low-quality retailing.

The term bonsai doesn't just refer to the plant. It can also be an adjective describing the process of dwarfing a plant while managing its growth. In order for your bonsai to have its own unique look, there are certain methods and techniques you must learn. It's also important to note that there are several bonsai styles you can create depending on the methods and techniques you use. This is why bonsai is also considered an art form—because you will be putting in your own creativity to shape your plant to reflect your personality.

If you're new to bonsai growing, you may want to start with an indoor plant. Indoor bonsai are more suitable for beginners since you won't have to deal with the climate outdoors. As long as the inside of your home has a consistent—and ideal—temperature, your bonsai will be just fine. Also, if you know anyone who has been growing bonsai as a hobby, you may ask for a starter tree that they have already trained. Such a tree would have already been introduced to this art form and prepared for this kind of growth. Also, such a tree would provide you with a pattern from which you can start making small and gradual adjustments. Of course, if you're not afraid of a challenge and you know that you have a green thumb, you may very well start your bonsai from a seed. It's really up to you!

Styles of Bonsai Plants

As years passed, there have been several styles of bonsai plants which have been created and discovered, all of which closely resemble the circumstances in nature. All of these styles are open to creativity and personal interpretation which means that the plants mustn't necessarily conform to these styles or any other form. Nevertheless, these styles can help you gain a better understanding of the varying bonsai shapes to help you in your bonsai training. Here are the most common styles of bonsai plants:

1. Bunjingi or Literati Style

You can find this style of tree in nature in densely populated areas where there are many other trees. In such a case, the trees are in fierce competition with each other, so they try to grow taller than all of the other trees. When growing your bonsai, allow the trunk to grow upward in a crooked manner without branching. To make your bonsai look tougher, you can remove the bark of the branches as well as from one side of the trunk. This style is typically grown in round-shaped, small pots and they're meant to show that the tree has struggled for its survival.

2. Chokkan or Formal Upright Style

This style is one of the most common and you can typically find it in nature as well, especially when trees receive a lot of sunlight and don't have to compete with other trees for resources. This style requires the tapering of the trunk that grows upright to be clearly visible. The trunk of such a bonsai must have a thick bottom and must grow thinner at the top.

3. Fukinagashi or Windswept Style

This style has a windswept look which shows the tree's struggle for survival. The trunk and branches of the bonsai would only grow to one side making it look like the wind has constantly blown the tree from one direction. Although the branches all grow out in different directions, you would bend them to one side.

4. Han Kengai or Semi-Cascade Style

In nature, you can find this style on cliffs as well as on the banks of lakes and rivers. When growing this style of bonsai, you must allow the trunk to grow upright for a bit then bend it sideways or downward. But this differs from the cascade style because the trunk of the bonsai will never grow below the bottom of its container.

5. Hokidachi or Broom Style

This style is suitable for deciduous trees which have fine and extensive branching. The trunk of the bonsai is upright and straight, but it doesn't continue all the way to the top. Instead, it branches out in different directions. The leaves and branches of the bonsai form a crown with a ball-shape.

6. Ikadabuki or Raft Style

There are some cases where cracked trees are still able to survive, and they do this by pointing their branches upward. The plant's old root system provides the branches with the nutrients the plant needs to survive. After some time, new roots will start to grow and eventually, this root system will take over the functions of the old one. The upward-pointing branches will grow into trunks with several branches and they will eventually contribute to a single canopy.

7. Ishisuki or Growing on Rock Style

For this style, the tree's roots would grow in the holes and cracks of a rock. Therefore, the root system doesn't have enough space to develop and start absorbing nutrients. Such plants will never really look healthy; they will always have the appearance that they're struggling for survival. When growing this style of bonsai, you must make sure to water and fertilize your plant often as there's no space for storing nutrients and water.

8. Kabudachi or Multi-Trunk Style

Theoretically, this style is the same as the Sokan style, but it has more trunks. All these trunks grow from one root system which means that essentially, it's just a single tree. All of the trunks form a single crown of leaves with the thickest trunk forming the top.

9. Kengai or Cascade Style

This style is inspired by trees in nature which grow on steep cliffs and bend downward because of a number of factors. This bonsai style can be a challenge to grow because it opposes the natural tendency of trees to grow in an upright direction. To ensure a downward growth, it's best to grow the bonsai in a tall pot. Allow your bonsai to grow upright for a bit then start bending it downward. Also, make sure the branches of the bonsai grow out horizontally to maintain the tree's balance.

10. Moyogi or Informal Upright Style

This is another common bonsai style that's also commonly found in nature. For this style, the trunk roughly grows in the shape of an "S" where branching occurs at every turn. Also, you must make sure that the tapering of the trunk for this style must be clearly visible.

11. Seki-Joju or Rock Planting Style

On rocky terrains, trees must search for soil that's rich in nutrients using their roots. This soil is usually found in holes and cracks. Until the roots reach the soil, they are vulnerable; thus, they need to keep themselves protected from the heat of the sun. In such a case, a special kind of bark grows around the roots of the trees. When growing this bonsai style, you would allow the roots of your plant to grow over a rock and into the container.

12. Shakkan or Leaning/Slanting Style

This style comes as a result of wind that often blows in a single direction or when trees grow in a shaded area, so they bend to access sunlight. In such cases, the tree will slant or lean in one direction. When growing this bonsai style, you should grow it at an angle between 60 and 80 degrees in relation to the ground. Make sure that the roots develop well on one side to ensure that the tree doesn't fall over. The trunk would be thicker at the bottom and can either be straight or slightly bent.

13. Sharimiki or Deadwood Style

Over time, some trees become barkless or bald in places due to extreme weather conditions. The bald spot typically starts at the area where the roots grow from the ground and the baldness grows thinner the more it continues up the tree's trunk. Sunlight then bleaches these barkless parts thus forming a unique look. When growing this style of bonsai, you would remove the bark using a sharp knife then treat the spots using calcium sulfate to hasten the process of bleaching.

14. Sokan or Double Trunk Style

This style is commonly found in nature but not as much in bonsai growing. Typically, both trunks would grow out of a single root system, but you can also grow the smaller trunk out of the bigger trunk. Both trunks vary in length and thickness. The trunk that is more developed grows upright while the less developed trunk grows slanted.

15. Yose-Ue or Forest/Group Planting Style

The appearance of this style is a lot similar to the Kabudachi style; however, instead of a single root system with several trunks, this is a group of trees growing together. For this style, you would use a large, shallow pot where you would place the most-developed trees at the center. All these trees are planted in a staggered pattern and they grow together to form a single crown of leaves.

Types of Bonsai Plants

Apart from the different styles of bonsai, there are also different types of bonsai plants you can choose from. These types work well with different styles and various growing conditions as well. When you've chosen the type of bonsai plant to grow, you may want to learn all that you can about it so you can grow it in the best possible way. Here are some of the most common types of bonsai plants to consider and some of their most notable characteristics:

1. **Apple**

    o   Part of the tropical bonsai tree varieties and is also called the Monkey Apple or Pitch Apple Bonsai Tree.

    o   When it blooms it has pink and white flowers. When the flowers fall off, small apple fruits grow in their place. They have aerial roots and dark-green leaves.

    o   Can be grown into different styles.

2. **Azalea**

    o   Has a one-of-a-kind appearance. Add both bloom and color to bonsai as an art form.

- When in bloom has white, red or pink flowers. Even without flowers, this bonsai has a striking appearance thanks to its extraordinary leaves.

- You can shape this bonsai into compact shrubbery much like other types of rhododendrons.

3. **Bahama Berry**

    - Also called Moujean Tea, Nashiainaguensis, "I Dry, I Die," and Pineapple Verbena.

    - It's not very attractive as a full-sized tree but when grown as a bonsai, the trunk has a twisty nature giving it an alluring and graceful appearance.

    - It's quite challenging to grow and it has a heavenly smell.

4. **Bald Cypress**

    - In nature, these trees grow in swampy, wet soils like those alongside flood plains and riverbanks. They can live up to a thousand years old.

BONSAI

- o In bonsai form, it has a more dome-like shape compared to the circular shape of those in nature.

- o Part of the deciduous tree varieties which means that its leaves all fall off during winter.

5. **Bamboo**

    - o A type of bamboo known as the "Nandina" is a domestic plant which is also called sacred or heavenly bamboo.

    - o It's not actually a tree, it's a miniature shrub.

    - o When merged with the bonsai practice, bamboo bonsai resembles the shape of a small bamboo tree.

6. **Black Olive**

    - o One of the most highly-valued types of bonsai. Has lush leaves along with a very intriguing pattern of growth.

    - o It flourishes in warm climates such as those in subtropical and tropical countries and has a very high salt tolerance.

    - o They don't lose their color no matter

what time of the year it is.

7. **Buddha's Ear**

    o   Belongs to the Alocasia Cucullata plant category and is also called Buddha's Hand, Chinese Taro, Buddha's First Lily, NaiHabarala, Buddha's Palm or Hooded Dwarf Elephant Tree.

    o   It produces small flowers which then grow into small berries.

    o   The leaves have a glossy structure with a heart shape.

8. **Bougainvillea**

    o   The plant has magnificent color and it blossoms into a woody vine.

BONSAI

- It can only flourish when you provide it with sufficient amounts of direct sunlight.

- It has enchanting blossoms which have a purple-pink color but interestingly enough, these are its leaves! The actual blossoms of this plant are quite small and have a yellow color.

9. **Boxwood**

    - This is one of the easiest types of bonsai to cultivate. You can shape this into different styles as the natural forms of this type of bonsai are easy to shape and twist into beautiful living statues.

    - When grown, the plant has a pom-pom-like appearance that's extremely appealing to the eyes.

    - There are over seventy different varieties of this type all of which are extremely sturdy.

10. **Bromeliad**

    - It possesses an intricate root system making it strikingly durable.

    - The coloration of the leaves vary widely adding an element of magic to the plant.

BONSAI

> Vivid colors varying from shades of green, gold, and maroon awaken the imagination. Some even have hued colors with cream, purple or red undertones.

- o The foliage that grows from this plant results in how you care for the tree — some leaves may be irregular and symmetrical or flat and broad.

11. Buttonwood

- o This type has a stunning artistic appearance though some consider it less attractive than other types.

- o You can shape this type to give it the appearance of a swan.

- o It's an excellent choice for those who want to nurture and coax bonsai into bloom.

12. Cactus Combo

- o It's extremely low-maintenance but it also has a unique type of beauty.

- o Growing this type means that you would be growing more than just one cactus plant at the same time.

BONSAI

- Only specific varieties of cacti can be used for this type of bonsai growing.

13. Cape Honeysuckle

- It has a rare kind of beauty which blossoms into a plant with stunning, vibrant hues.

- Both the blossoms and the foliage of the plant have dazzling coloration.

- When growing this type of bonsai, make

sure it gets enough sunlight for it to survive.

14. Cedar

- It has short needles that gather in clusters

growing sparsely along its branches.

- o It's a very rare type of bonsai which requires a lot of in-depth care.
- o It's easy to style and shape, making it one of the most rewarding types of plants to grow.

15. Cherry Blossom

- o It's a part of the "prunus" family of trees which includes more than 430 different varieties of trees.
- o Also called Hill Cherry, Oriental Cherry, and Japanese Cherry.
- o The plant is native to Asia, specifically in Korea, Japan, and China.

16. Cherry

- o You can grow this from a cherry seed, but you can also purchase specialized cherry seeds from reputable sources.
- o It's best to use a one-gallon container for growing this bonsai.
- o It's quite challenging to grow this type of tree making it suitable for those who already have experience growing bonsai.

17. Chinese Elm

- This is one of the most attractive types thanks to the gorgeous contrast between its twisting trunk and its small leaves.

- The structure of this bonsai is considered visually pleasing and exotic with its thick and sturdy trunk combined with the delicate branches.

- It flourishes in warmer climates and it's better to be grown indoors.

18. Crepe Myrtle

- This is one of the more interesting types of bonsai with its crepe-like blossoms and the bark that sheds from one season to another in a range of colors.

- It's native to Australia and Asia and has deciduous leaves which means they will fall off during winter.

- This type of bonsai requires a lot of sunlight to nurture it and allow the flowers to bloom.

19. Dogwood

- A charming type of bonsai that takes pruning and training well making it an excellent choice for beginner bonsai growers.

- It has deep-green leaves which go through shades of red and purple during autumn.

- It sprouts enchanting flowers during spring that have a sweet scent much like perfume.

20. Ficus

- There are around 850 different varieties of Ficus trees.

- Most of these varieties take pruning elegantly and they are easy to care for, even with the restrictions of bonsai growth.

- It should only be grown indoors near a window, so it gets enough sunlight.

21. Fukien Tea

- This is one of the most difficult types of bonsai to grow thus making it more suitable to seasoned bonsai growers.

- Cultivating and maintaining this type of bonsai requires very specific skills.

- Pruning is also a challenge unless you have adequate knowledge of how to do it properly.

22. Ginkgo

- This type is well-known all over the world because of its medicinal properties and the unique shape of its leaves.

- It's a singular tree specimen which doesn't have any close relatives.

- It can thrive on rocky terrains and other types of harsh terrains making it quite easy to grow and cultivate.

23. Ginseng Ficus

- This tree has an unusual appearance but has a very high resistance.
- Its sturdiness makes it suitable for beginners.
- It has a thick trunk with interesting curves and twists along with dense foliage at the top.

24. Grapevine

- This type of bonsai grows in the form of a bushy tree.
- It has a vigorous growth pattern and the size it reaches is only limited by your maintenance and taste.
- This type requires a lot of care and high-maintenance in order for it to thrive and flourish.

25. Green Mound Juniper

- It has a visual appeal like no other with its gorgeous green leaves and the different designs and shapes you can apply to its trunk.
- This is relatively easy to grow and cultivate compared to other types of

bonsai trees.

- It can survive in different kinds of temperatures, which means that you can grow it either outdoors or indoors.

26. Hibiscus

- It has an incredibly unique appearance with different colored flowers ranging from white, yellow, purple, red, and more.

- The flowers of this tree remain throughout the entire growing season.

- It's a rare and exotic type of bonsai that can be a challenge to grow successfully.

27. Himalayan Cedar

- It has a wonderfully unique scent which people consider highly therapeutic to de-stress the body and mind.

- Once the green-colored needles of this plant sprout, they show golden undertones giving the tree a gorgeous appearance.

- This is a conical-like plant that needs a lot of regular trimming, so it doesn't grow beyond the desired height.

28. Jade

- This is a low-maintenance type of bonsai that belongs to the Succulents family.

- The leaves of this plant has the ability to store large amounts of water for a long period of time.

- The stems of this tree are thick and have an elegant brown color.

29. Japanese Black Pine

BONSAI

- This is one of the most popular and highly-values types of bonsai plants.

- The leaves are extremely delicate and have a needle-like shape which grow in pairs.

- During the spring, the plant blooms small red-colored flowers and when they fall off, small brown cones grow in their place.

30. Japanese Maple

- This is a very popular type of bonsai thanks to the plant's striking beauty, especially during autumn.

- The leaves have hues of orange, red, and yellow which will light up any room with vitality and color.

- It's suitable for beginners because it's easy to grow—you don't need to spend a lot of time, care, and maintenance for such a

BONSAI

bonsai.

31. Juniper

- This type is quite easy to find on the market, making it one of the most commonly grown types in the world.

- It's a beautiful plant which has different varieties for you to choose from.

- As long as you give this plant enough light and water, you can grow this bonsai in virtually any conditions both outdoors and indoors.

32. Liquidambar

- This is the best type of tree for those who like colors as it changes its colors as the seasons change.

- The structure of this plant is strikingly pretty and in autumn it turns shades of burgundy-purple, dazzling red, and bright orange.

- This type requires cold temperatures for it to thrive and produce the much-anticipated shades of leaves.

33. Mimosa

- This is a delicate, elegant, and beautiful bonsai type with unique pom-pom like flowers.

- It also has delicate fronds that have a fern-like appearance covered in several small leaves which, when touched, feel soft and light.

- This type has a rapid growth rate making

bonsai training and sculpting much easier.

34. Money Tree

o   This tree symbolizes luck and prosperity. People believe that growing this bonsai brings wealthy harmony.

- It is also called Jade Tree, Provision Tree, Guiana Chestnut, Saba Nut, Malabar Chestnut, and Pimpo.

- This tree can be grown both outdoors and indoors as long as the plant gets a lot of warmth and sunlight.

35. Needle Juniper

- This is suitable for both beginners and seasoned bonsai growers.

- It's easy to train, prune, grow, and cultivate. You can even shape the tree to resemble a very old tree to make it even more appealing.

- There are several species of this type of tree available.

36. Oak

- This is part of the Quercus family which includes hundreds of other types of trees.

- It has a lovely appearance making it quite gratifying to grow and contemplate once it's fully grown.

- You need to be careful when pruning the roots of this plant as it needs a very specific method of pruning.

37. Pine

- This has an aged appearance and an intricate form that has the potential to alter the mind and reward you as a grower in various ways.

- However, this isn't an easy type of bonsai to grow and cultivate so you may want to try the easier types first.

- This is another popular type thanks to its classical aesthetics and evergreen needles which remain all throughout the year.

38. Pomegranate

- o This is an intriguing specimen even though it doesn't produce bright colors in autumn.

- o During spring, striking flowers start to bloom on the branches of the plant after which small fruits grow in their place.

- o This is a rare and exotic plant with a lovely twisted trunk that provides an aged and gnarled appearance.

39. Powder Puff

- o This type has a one-of-a-kind appearance which most consider whimsical.

- o It has showy flowers that are mesmerizing, delightful, and look like puffy cotton balls.

- o You can shape this type of bonsai into different designs making it look like a stunning living sculpture.

40. Privet

- o This is an ideal choice for hobbyist bonsai growers with their shrubby shape and

BONSAI

lovely appearance.

- o For this type, it's easy to prune, trim, and perform other bonsai techniques as it grows.
- o It's a very sturdy type of bonsai and it's also very adaptive.

41. Pyracantha

- o This is actually a shrub, not a tree that possesses thorns.
- o You need to trim this bonsai regularly as it can grow quite rapidly.
- o Apart from the lovely evergreen leaves, the plant also produces white flowers during the spring season and when these fall off, small orange or red berries grow in their place.

42. Redwood

- o The majestic and rare beauty of this bonsai has made it a symbol of authenticity and strength in nature.
- o This type of bonsai is extremely hardy and evergreen leaves are truly a joy to observe.

- This is a relatively low-maintenance plant that both beginners and seasoned bonsai growers can enjoy.

43. Rosemary

- This type grows fast and is very sturdy.
- When pruning this type of bonsai, you can use the parts which you've cut as an ingredient for cooking.
- For other people, they believe that this plant grant prosperity and luck to their growers.

44. Sea Grape

- This type of bonsai has a lovely shape and delicate flowers with ivory color.
- It's suitable to grow this plant outdoors, especially if you want the plant to bear fruit.
- The plant has stunning leathery leaves with a round shape that have a red vein running through their whole base.

45. Serissa

- This exotic type of bonsai has ever-present flowers that make the whole plant visually appealing.

- The foliage is vital-green in color, glossy, and has spiny branches that make up the dome-like canopy.

- It's easy to train and shape this plant into an endless array of designs but it does require a good amount of attention and care.

46. Trident Maple

- This is another type of bonsai that's extremely sturdy that it's able to withstand harsh conditions.

- It has a majestic look to it, and it can even survive after severe pruning.

- This plant has a very high rate of growth which means that you would have to trim it regularly.

47. Weeping Willow

- This type of bonsai is mesmerizingly beautiful making it one of the most popular types grown all over the world.

- The branches of this plant have a very striking shape with small catkins that start out with a graceful silver color which turns creamy white as the plant matures.

- It lasts for up to twenty-five years as long as you care for it well and you maintain it properly.

48. Wisteria

- This type can thrive and grow in different parts of the world.

- It has a whimsical appearance to it — even though it's a shrub, a fully-grown bonsai looks like a miniature tree in bloom.

- One incredible characteristic of this bonsai is that its flowers won't start blooming until ten years after you've started cultivating it.

49. Zelkova

- This type is easy to grow, making it suitable even for amateur bonsai growers.

- It's highly-resistant, especially in terms of plant diseases.

- It's a very sturdy type of plant with branches that create a lovely crown with an arc-shape.

Choosing Your Bonsai

When it comes to choosing your bonsai, it doesn't end with the type of bonsai you want. There are other factors to consider as well. Although most people would like to choose their plant depending on its aesthetic appeal, this isn't the best way to go about it. If you really want to select the best plant for yourself, consider these other factors as well:

- Size

Think about where you plan to place your bonsai. These plants come in a wide range of sizes; therefore, you must choose one that will fit into the space you plan to put it in. For instance, if you want to place your bonsai on your desk at work, you may want to go for one of the smaller varieties. But if you want to place your bonsai in a bigger space, then you have the option to choose a plant that can grow a bit taller or bigger.

- Environment

Think about whether you plan to place your bonsai indoors or outdoors. Generally, indoor plants are easier to deal with, especially when you keep a constant temperature inside your home or office. But if you plan to grow an outdoor bonsai, then you have to be more careful with your choice. Later on, we will be discussing more about caring for indoor and outdoor bonsai to help you determine which is more suitable for you.

- Your bonsai growing experience

We have already gone through the different types of bonsai. If there is one thing you should take away from learning about the different types of bonsai, it is that some types are easier to grow compared to others. If this is your first time to grow bonsai, it's recommended to choose types which are easy to grow, and which don't require a lot of maintenance. This will give you a better idea of how growing bonsai actually works, how much time and effort you need to put into the process, and all the other processes involved in growing bonsai. After growing your first bonsai, you may choose to grow another (or several others). This is the time when you may opt for bonsai types which are more challenging to grow and cultivate.

- Purchasing a healthy starter plant

Finally, if you plan to purchase a starter plant instead of growing your bonsai from seed, make sure you choose a healthy plant. Here are some tips to help you choose:

  o Healthy bonsai must have **branches** which are evenly distributed throughout the whole shape.

  o Healthy bonsai must have **leaves** with a healthy, bright-green color.

  o Healthy bonsai must have **roots** which stick out of the soil slightly but must be securely anchored into the container.

  o Healthy bonsai must have a **trunk** that's thick at the bottom while growing increasingly thinner as it reaches the top.

CHAPTER 3

PREPARING TO GROW YOUR BONSAI

The art of bonsai is famous all over the world. The first time a person sees a real bonsai, it evokes feelings of curiosity and mystery. While most people lose interest in bonsai after some time, others feel compelled to learn more about these miniature wonders even to the point of growing one themselves. However, growing bonsai doesn't just require specific gardening skills. The art can be therapeutic, and it also enables growers to become more fortuitous and patient.

Growing bonsai is a relaxing hobby that you can maintain for as long as you can keep your bonsai alive. As a matter of fact, the ancient Chinese people had a belief that the souls of those able to care for their bonsai for a long time would be granted eternity. This belief comes from another belief that trees can connect human beings to holiness — and they are the connection between earth and heaven.

Before learning how to actually grow bonsai, you must first think about the type of tree you want to plant, the growing environment you plan to place your bonsai in, and the climate in your area. There are certain types of bonsai that are recommended for beginners, so if you're a first-time bonsai grower, you may choose these types. Also, choose those that are easy to shape and train to enable you to practice the most basic bonsai growing techniques without difficulty.

Maintaining a healthy and strong bonsai requires a lot of care and attention. If you make the choice to grow your own bonsai, the key to success is doing it right. Over time, you will start seeing your bonsai grow and flourish, and this is when you will experience that sense of accomplishment. Maintaining bonsai is a long process. In fact, it will never end for as long as your bonsai continues living. In some countries — like China and Japan — the elderly pass on their bonsai plants to younger generations to continue caring for them.

Growing a Bonsai from a Seed

Although it's easier for beginners to purchase starter or partially-grown bonsai to begin their bonsai-growing journey, you also have the option to grow bonsai from seeds. Although this is a slow process, growing bonsai from a seed is much more rewarding, especially as you see your seed grow into a beautiful tree thanks to the time, effort, and care you put into it. Depending on the type of bonsai you plan to grow, you may have to wait for a couple of months to witness germination. There are even some types of bonsai which may need a few seasonal changes before the plant can break out of the seed coat. Growing a bonsai from a seed, caring for it, shaping it properly, and styling it in a unique way will ensure that you have a plant that is truly one-of-a-kind. If you plan to take on this long process, here are some tips for you:

- Obtaining the seed

Have you ever thought about how or where you can obtain seeds for bonsai growing? The fact is, you can collect any seed from your surroundings. But you can also purchase the seed from an online store or your local gardening shop. Just stay away from shops that offer "bonsai tree seeds" because there are no such things. Bonsai grow from the same seeds as normal trees. Here are some points to guide you when it comes to obtaining the seed:

- If you plan to obtain the seeds from your surroundings, the best time to do so is in autumn. This is the best time to plant the seeds as well.

- If you plan to plant the seeds when it's not their season to grow, you must perform a process known as stratification. This involves treating the seed in order to mimic the natural weather conditions it requires before germination. This is a fairly complex process, so it's not recommended for beginners.

- If you plan to purchase your seeds online, you must do some research first. Read the reviews of various online shops to see which ones are most reliable and trusted. Also, you may want to contact the seller first before making your final choice.

- Whether you plan to purchase seeds online or in a local gardening shop, you may want to opt for those which offer seeds that are certified disease-free. Such seeds have been specially treated and bred to be resistant to the most common bonsai diseases. This makes it easier for you to grow your bonsai from seed.

- Learning about stratification and scarification

There are some seeds that must first undergo stratification before they can germinate. A process known as cold stratification involves a moist period and a cold state the seeds go through during the winter season. These seeds are the ones that fall to the ground during the autumn season. Then they spend the winter months on the ground before they start growing. When spring comes, it brings warmer weather which, in turn, triggers the germination process.

If you're planning to plant a seed which requires cold stratification, you must mimic this process first. The easiest way to do this is by filling a plastic bag with potting soil, placing the seed in it, then placing the bag in your refrigerator for a certain number of months. This allows the seeds to germinate. After germination, you can transfer the seeds to your bonsai container.

There is also a process known as scarification wherein you would soak the seeds in water for a certain amount of time, usually within one to two days. This is recommended for seeds that possess very hard shells or coatings. Some people choose to scratch or file the shell using a needle or pin to help hasten the process. Certain types of seeds can be scarified. These seeds are naturally designed to only germinate under very specific conditions. For instance, there are those that must first be exposed to fire before they germinate, while there are others that must first pass through the digestive tract of animals. For these types of seeds, you may have to break the shell down yourself to allow for germination.

- Helping your seed germinate

If you want to grow your own bonsai from a seed, the best thing to do is plant several seeds. Simply planting a single seed might not yield results, especially if you're new to growing bonsai. Labeling your seeds is key to help you see which seeds are thriving and which ones aren't. Label your seeds every step of the way. Include the date when you planted them, the type of plant, the processes you have performed on them, and other important information.

Whether you have chosen to plant only one type of tree or several types, it's important to do as much research as you can about them. That way, you will be equipped with the proper knowledge and specific recommendations for the type of trees you have chosen. Germinating seeds is a long and arduous process. You much check your seeds regularly, especially if you've kept them in your refrigerator. As soon as the seeds have germinated, take them out and place them in a pot or container.

- Caring for your germinated seed

Some seeds germinate faster than others. But as soon as your seeds have germinated and they have developed true leaves, you can feel more confident about your plant's chances of survival. When your bonsai trees outgrow seedling trays, you may transfer them to bigger containers or pots. Just make sure to pull out the whole tree including the root system, so you don't cause any damage. After this, you can start caring for your bonsai as a regular bonsai. There will be more on this later.

Selecting a Healthy Starter Bonsai

If this is your first time to grow bonsai, you might feel like you can't grow one from a seed. You're not alone. A lot of beginners opt to begin their bonsai growing journey with a starter bonsai as this is much easier. Just like regular trees, bonsais live for a long, long time. That is as long as the grower takes good care of the plant. The lifespan of a bonsai would depend on other factors as well such as the type of tree and its growing conditions or environment.

All types of bonsai trees require maintenance

although some require more maintenance than others. For beginners, it's recommended to choose a type of bonsai that's easy to care for and doesn't require a lot of maintenance. Also, remember that various tree types grow and thrive better in specific regions. This is why it's important to do research before making a final choice in terms of the type of bonsai you want to grow.

Purchasing your first starter bonsai tree can be quite a daunting task. You may purchase the starter tree online or get one from your local garden center or nursery. The latter is more recommended because you will be able to get a tree that you know will grow well in your area and you can also ask for advice from the seller. Here are more tips to help you choose your first starter tree:

- Aside from the climate in your area, also consider the growing conditions of the tree. Do you plan to keep it outdoors or indoors? How much sunlight will the tree be exposed to in the location you plan to place it in? In some cases, you might even need to use grow lights if you plan to grow your bonsai indoors.

- Make sure to choose a healthy tree from the beginning. Ask help from the seller to help you find a healthy starter tree. To give you a better idea of what to look out for, here are some pointers:

- Check to make sure that the tree doesn't have any bugs or pests on it. Check all the parts of the tree to make sure.

- The tree should have sturdy branches and its trunk should be significantly thicker than its branches.

- Speaking of the trunk, it should not be too straight unless you want to grow a bonsai with a formal upright position.

- Check the health of the tree's roots by checking whether it is firm and secure in the container.

Choosing the Perfect Pot for Your Bonsai

A bonsai cannot truly become a bonsai without its pot. Combining your bonsai with the perfect pot will create a special kind of harmony, and that is part of the art of bonsai. There are many types of containers that can serve as the pot for your bonsai as long as they meet specific requirements namely:

- It must have drainage holes.

BONSAI

- It must have wiring holes so you can fix the tree to the pot.

- It may be made of concrete, plastic, ceramic, and metals which don't release toxins. You can even make your own pot if you have the skills to do so.

But the best type of bonsai pot to use is one made of porcelain or ceramic which has been stoneware burned. This type of pot is healthy for bonsai because it absorbs water but doesn't store water within the material.

When choosing the pot for your bonsai, always prioritize the plant's health and safety. Mature bonsai have to undergo years of bonsai training to help their root systems adapt to small pots. Growing bonsai requires perseverance and patience, and these virtues will also come into play when you're choosing the perfect pot. One of the most important factors to consider is the appropriate measurement, especially in terms of depth. It should be deep enough to support the entire root system of the bonsai. Here are the other factors for you to consider:

1. The style of the pot

First, think about whether you want a pot with a masculine design or one with a feminine design. Bonsai trees typically have a mixture of masculine and feminine aspects so you can emphasize the dominance through the style of the pot. You can also use the attributes of the plant you plan to grow to help you choose the pot. Bonsai trees which are considered more feminine are those that have grace, curves, sparse branches, and smooth bark. On the other hand, bonsai trees that are considered more masculine are those that have thick trunks, dense branches, old bark, deadwood, and those which have a strong appearance.

2. The design of the pot

Of course, the pot's design should match the style you've chosen. The more the style, design, and appearance of your bonsai match, the more harmonious your bonsai growing experience will be. Some common pot design options are rectangular, round, angular, oval, convex or concave. Masculine pots are deeper, more angular, and have clean lines. Feminine pots are more delicate, have soft lines, and are fairly sleek and low.

In terms of the glaze of the pot, it's best to make sure that the color you choose must appear in the bonsai itself. Whether the color appears in the flowers, leaves, fruit or bark of the tree, choose the color wisely. Basically, the goal here is to create balance and harmony for your bonsai. You may go online and look for samples of bonsai in pots and see which ones you would like to emulate. You can also use these as your inspiration for choosing the perfect pot for your own bonsai.

3. The size of the pot

When it comes to the size of the pot, the general rule of thumb is that the pot should have the same height at the bonsai's trunk's width above the nebari. Pots that have a rectangular or oval shape are typically 2/3 of the bonsai's height. Pots that have a square or round shape are typically 1/3 of the bonsai's height.

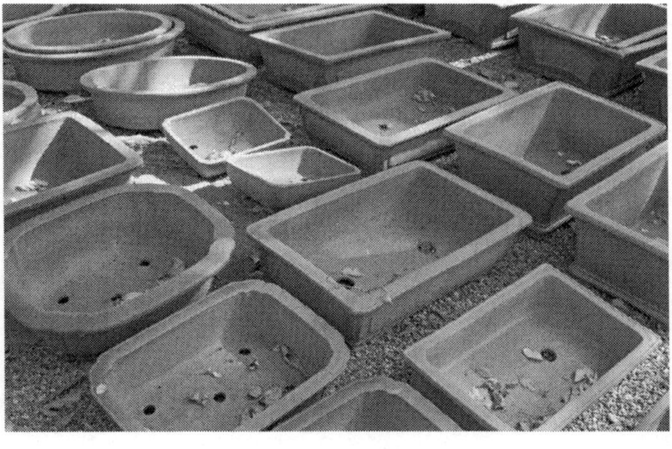

CHAPTER 4

GROWING BASICS

Just because bonsai is considered an art form, and the process has been refined and studies for centuries, this should intimidate you so much that you don't want to try it for yourself. The fact is, with the right knowledge and skills, virtually anyone can learn how to cultivate and grow bonsai in their homes. As long as you choose the right tree for yourself and the perfect pot for your tree, you'll be well on your way towards growing your own miniature tree.

So, how do you create your own bonsai? The very first step is to obtain a starter tree (or a seed if you think you can grow a bonsai from seed) and start cultivating it. We've already discussed the fundamentals of choosing the perfect tree. By the time you have made a final choice of what type of bonsai tree to grow, this means that you should have already learned everything you can about the specific type of bonsai as well as the special recommendations for it. This should also mean that you had taken into consideration all the factors we have discussed before you picked the species to grow.

To make things easier for you, there are bonsai starter kits available in gardening shops and online shops. These can help you learn more about bonsai growing along with other helpful information such as the techniques to use for the cultivation and customization of your bonsai. Normally, it would take a few years before you can start shaping and styling your tree. But learning about these techniques early on can help you prepare for when it's time for you to do them.

Growing bonsai isn't as simple as growing other types of plants in your garden. It involves various processes, methods, and techniques each of which we will be discussing in the next few chapters. But before going into the details of these techniques, let's start with the basics.

Basic Tools You Need for Growing Your Bonsai

Just as there are special skills and techniques needed for growing bonsai, there are also special tools you need for the task. The proper equipment is essential for growing, cultivating, training, and caring for your bonsai. With these basic tools and equipment, you can do whatever you want and whatever your tree needs for you to achieve that perfect bonsai look you're dreaming of. As a beginner, it's recommended to purchase the most basic tools at the beginning. Then the longer you work with your bonsai, the more you can start investing in specialized tools and equipment. Let's go through these tools now:

1. Bending and Protective Tools

In cases where you need to bend the trunk or branches of your bonsai heavily, you must take protective measures to avoid tearing the bark, breaking the wood, and to help with the healing of small fissures and cracks that may result from bending. Most people use **wet raffia** to tightly wrap around the area you plan to bend before applying the wire. You may also use **bicycle tube** or **fusing rubber tape** for the same purpose. For the parts of your plant where you plan to attach guy or fixation wires, you can protect them by wrapping them with **infusion or fish tank hoses**. For bending heavily, you can use ergonomically designed tools like **rubber-padded steel levers** and **special screw clamps** that come in different sizes and shapes. For bending sturdy trunks, **iron rebars** can be very useful too.

2. Deadwood Tools

The primary purpose of working on deadwood is to make it look as natural as possible without evidence of human intervention. As paradoxical as this may seem, there are several tools you can use for this purpose such as:

- A **branch splitter** is a type of sharp pliers meant for splitting multiple dead stumps and branches.//
- A **jin plier** can be used to break off tiny particles of wood or to pull fibers.
- A **slim chisel** can be used to lift wood fibers.
- **Carving hooks** and **loop knives** can be used to peel the bark off or to carve slight furrows.
- Sets of **carving tools** can be used for different tasks such as hollowing out, narrowing, smoothing, shaping or contouring deadwood.
- A **gas torch** can be used to remove fibers that stick out and to eliminate any trace of your work. Then you can use **nylon, steel or brass brushes** to brush off the layer of charred wood.
- For the preservation of decayed

deadwood, **wood hardener** is the best to use.

3. Electric Tools

When you think there is a need to use electric tools or power tools, make sure you know how to use these properly and safely. You need extreme caution when working with such tools in order to avoid injuries while working on your bonsai. Also, when working with electric tools, concentrate fully on the task and make sure you're alert and awake while you work. Although you may not need these tools as a beginner bonsai grower, it's still a good idea to be aware of what they are. Some of the basic examples of electric tools include:

- angled carving hook
- branch splitter
- carving tools
- curved scalpel
- cut carving tools
- "Dremel 300" machine with various Dremel bits
- gas torch
- jin liquid

- "Makita GD 800C" die grinder
- protective glasses
- round carving hook
- small carving tools
- small loop knife
- spear plough
- strong, straight scalpel
- various circular brushes
- various grinders
- various screw wrenches

4. Knives and Saws

You need these tools for cutting trunks, roots or branches of your bonsai which are either too hard or too thick for pliers or shears. You must also know how to use these properly, so you don't end up bending or breaking them. In order to smooth the wounds and cuts left by saws and pliers, you can use a grafting knife just like the professionals. Some basic examples of these tools are:

- grafting knife
- medium-sized or large foldable saw

- sickle knife
- sickle saw
- thin pruning saw

5. Maintenance Tools

For when you need to remove dirt and rust that has accumulated on the blades of your tools, you can use **rust erasers**. For when you need to sharpen your blades, you may use **grindstones** which are available in different types. For maintaining blades and hinges, you may use **camellia oil** or **gun oil**. You may also want to have **coco brushes** on-hand to sweep up soil surfaces, trunks, tools, and more.

6. Pliers and Shears

There are many different types of pliers available in varying sizes as well. For instance, you need concave cutters to remove branches from your bonsai's trunk where you want to have deeper cuts which won't leave a scar after healing. Such cutters come with different kinds of blades for different kinds of cuts.

Shears also come in various shapes and sizes. You can use these for cutting small branches, leaves, roots or twigs. If you plan to grow a small type of bonsai, purchase pliers and shears that will suit your plant's size. Some basic examples of pliers and shears include:

- azalea and shohin shears
- jin or wire bending plier
- knob cutter
- leaf cutter
- long slim twig shears
- pruning shears
- root plier
- small or large concave cutter with straight blades
- small or large wire cutter
- standard shears
- standard strong shears (for root pruning)

7. Repotting Tools and for Working on Roots

When you need to remove your bonsai's root ball, you need to use special **sickle knives** and **sickle saws** to cut along the pot's interior. For this task, solid angular bowls made of plastic make your work cleaner, more comfortable, and easier. Other tools for repotting and rootwork include **root rakes** and **root hooks** which come in different variants and sizes. When it comes to pruning roots, you can use a standard pair of strong shears with a solid handle and strong blades. There are also **soil scoops** available in varying sizes that you can use to scoop and pour soil. For removing weeds, applying moss, and performing other tasks, a **tweezer spatula** will come in handy.

8. Wiring Tools

When it comes to wiring bonsai, you need **wire** with different diameters, pliers to bend the wire, and a **wire cutter**. These are the basic tools needed which also come in various sizes and shapes. For the wire, the easiest to apply is aluminum, but copper works well too.

9. Watering Tools

The most basic tool for watering is a **watering can** which comes in all sizes and shapes. But for bonsai, it's best to choose one with a long neck and a fine nozzle. Other watering tools include a **ball-shower** for when you need to water a couple of trees. For a larger collection of bonsai trees, you may go with a **garden hose with a built-in sprinkler stick**. You may also need **spray cans** to spray your bonsai with plant products like fertilizers or to mist your plant once in a while. There are also **watering systems** available which water your bonsais automatically at a set time. Of course, these are more advisable for when you have many plants to care for.

BONSAI

Basic Care Tips for Growing Bonsai

A bonsai is a fun and relaxing plant to have in your home or office. Although growing bonsai requires a lot of time, attention, and effort, all of these will well be worth it. If this is your first time to grow bonsai, it's recommended to learn all that you can about the different aspects of this process. That way, you will have a better idea of what to do when you're already growing the plant. To start you off, here are some basic tips for you:

- Where to place your bonsai

No matter where you place your bonsai, it will surely bring a natural calming feel to your space. It will add an enchanting element to your home, office or even outdoors. Just be sure that the location of your bonsai allows it to bask in direct sunlight regularly, so it won't wither away.

For you to determine the best place to display your miniature tree, you should first know the type of plant you have and whether it's more suitable to grow outdoors or indoors. Outdoor bonsai thrive well when they get a lot of sunlight and when they are exposed to the changing of the seasons. Indoor bonsai thrive well in stable temperatures all year long.

After determining the type of bonsai you have and whether you should place it inside or outside of your home, finding the best location is relatively simple. Here are some general tips for you which apply to most types of bonsais:

- When it comes to **positioning**, make sure to keep your bonsai away from drafts or direct heat.

- When it comes to **lighting**, make sure to keep your bonsai in an area where it can get a lot of sunlight.

- When it comes to **humidity**, make sure your bonsai gets enough to keep the soil moist.

- Finding the right soil

When it comes to the soil for your bonsai, you must find a type of soil that can retain some water but also drains quickly. It must also contain tiny particles which help aerate the soil in order for the roots to gain access to oxygen. You can find specialty soils online or in your local gardening shop for your bonsai. Make sure to choose the right soil for your plant to survive and grow into a healthy tree.

- Watering your bonsai

Although this is one of the most obvious things to do for your bonsai, watering bonsai isn't the same as watering other types of plants. There are specific requirements and steps to water your bonsai properly in order to maintain its health.

- Pruning your bonsai

The main goal of pruning bonsai is to help maintain the shape you want your plant to have as it is growing. Pruning is also essential as it ensures the continuous growth of the bonsai tree. There are specific tools to use for pruning your bonsai to keep you from causing damage to any of its parts. Also, you should first think about what shape or style you want your bonsai to have, so you can prune it accordingly.

- Repotting your bonsai

This is an important aspect of bonsai growing. The goal of repotting bonsai is for the removal of excess roots that may cause the bonsai's starvation. Also, repotting your bonsai ensures that it can keep growing in its small container. It's important to repot your bonsai at least one time every two years or so depending on the growth rate of your bonsai.

- Finding support

Finally, one of the basic things you can do when growing bonsai is to find support—this means connecting with other bonsai growers. Being able to communicate with other people who grow bonsai, especially the ones who have been growing bonsai longer than you have allows you to learn more about the journey you've begun. This is also a fun way to connect with other people as you share your experiences, tips, and mistakes you have done and learned from.

Styling and Shaping Techniques

You may have already admired different types of bonsai from afar which is why you've made the choice to grow your own tiny tree. Two important aspects of being able to grow bonsai successfully are careful styling and shaping the tree to the form you want it to have. The techniques you would use for these tasks are the ones which make bonsai and art form—and these techniques require a lot of patience and attention to detail.

When it comes to styling and shaping bonsai, there are several things to consider. From the start, you must make sure that your tree has a strong foundation. To do this, you must focus on the growth of the bonsai's root system and its trunk. If these parts of your bonsai are sturdy and healthy, you won't have to worry about damaging your plant when it's time for shaping and styling.

Be very careful when choosing the part of your bonsai that you want to shape or style and which part

BONSAI

you'd like to grow naturally. This will help you make successful changes to your bonsai accordingly. Here are some tips for you:

1. Shaping the roots of your bonsai

The whole root system of a bonsai consists of the underground structure and the roots which are exposed on the surface. The latter are known as the "nebari." Cultivating healthy nebari is essential to the proper growth of your bonsai and to give it a true bonsai appearance. If you have decided to purchase an older plant as your first bonsai, there are special steps you must take in order to re-shape the nebari, especially if they haven't been maintained well in the past. In such a case, you may have to prune the sub-surface roots to ensure optimal growth. But if you start growing your bonsai from seed or you've purchased a starter plant, you can start working on the nebari sooner.

As aforementioned, you would have to repot your bonsai regularly as it grows. This is the perfect time for you to prune the nebari of your bonsai. But before you start pruning, you must first make sure that the nebari are spaced evenly, healthy, and they are growing well. Also, it's only recommended to prune the parts of the nebari that aren't necessary such as the outgrowths. Each time you repot your bonsai, prune the nebari in order to shape it well.

Here are the methods to use when shaping the nebari:

- Cutting

This involves cutting off the unnecessary and undesirable parts of the nebari including the phloem, bark, and cambium. However, be careful not to cut too deep that you would reach the root's structure. After cutting, leave your plant alone for some time to allow the roots to continue growing.

- Air Layering

This also involves the removal of the phloem, bark, and cambium of your bonsai. But instead of leaving your plant alone after, air layering involves wrapping the open roots to retain their moisture. Most people use moistened sphagnum moss as wrapping. Over time, new roots start growing on the wrapped surface. This is an excellent method to promote the development of roots; however, it can be quite a challenge to maintain.

- Grafting

For this method, you can perform it on its own or combine it with the other two methods. Grafting involves attaching a bonsai tree with the same species to a mature bonsai tree in the area where you want to promote the growth of roots. Over time, the younger plant will take root in the area.

2. Shaping the trunk of your bonsai

The term "kokejun" refers to the taper of the bonsai's trunk. Ideally, the trunk should have a thick base with even tapering towards the center and top. Since bonsai can't achieve this naturally, you have to guide and train your bonsai for it to grow this way. Growing bonsai requires an increase in the thickening of the trunk and tapering. You can do this by improving its "tachiagari"—the bonsai's initial growth and rise. And the best way to do this is by pruning carefully.

Also, you must consider the curves of your bonsai's trunk as well as the refinements of its form. Think about the form you want your bonsai to have so you can plan how to achieve it as your bonsai is growing. From the location of the branches to the distribution of foliage, leaf reduction and more, planning must start from the beginning while you still have a young tree with a pliable trunk. Here are the basic forms of bonsai which you may consider:

- Bunjingi

This is also known as a bonsai's literati form and it's based on the definite line the tree forms. The foliage, limbs, and trunk of the bonsai would have to be trained to emphasize the line by following it. This form differs from the others in a very subtle way though it does have a very prominent trunk.

- Chokkan

This is the most traditional form of bonsai and it's considered aesthetically natural because this is how trees usually look like in nature. Even if your bonsai has an organic form, you still need to pay attention to its growth and train it carefully as it is growing.

- Moyohgi

This form is almost identical to chokkan but it's more informal. It has an upright form but it's not as symmetrical. For this, the trunk of the bonsai may be tilted slightly while still maintaining a basic vertical structure.

- Shakan

This form of bonsai is slanting and for a bonsai to achieve this, it must have a prominent and sturdy nebari growing on one side of it. Creating this form requires special planning. You need to start training your bonsai as its roots are still developing actively.

After deciding the form of your bonsai, you can start crafting its kokejun. For this process, there are different methods you can employ namely:

- Tachiagari Cultivation

BONSAI

The development of tachiagari is increased when new limbs grow from the bonsai's trunk. These extra branches promote the growth of the whole tree as they force more nutrients and water to the bonsai's trunk and roots. When you remove the branches, you are also removing this extra nutrient and water flow. Hence, if you allow the limbs to remain there, this helps the trunk to become stronger and thicker too.

- Repeated Pruning

In order to develop kokejun, you must allow the limbs of your bonsai to grow. For this method, you would prune the buds of your bonsai repeatedly in order to boost the growth of the trunk. The best times to prune are late autumn and early summer. Then you may shape the trunk using wire as it grows thicker. You can start training the trunk of your bonsai two months after it has started budding early in the summer. However, this method is an arduous one which takes a long time to achieve.

- Tate-Kae

For this method, you would develop the kokejun by pruning a bonsai's trunk selectively. In doing this, you would encourage a new limb to grow which, in turn, becomes thicker and starts to merge with the trunk. To do this, prune the trunk right above the branch you have chosen.

BONSAI

CHAPTER 5

PLANTING AND REPOTTING

Now that we've covered the basics, it's time to start tackling the different processes and techniques involved in bonsai growing one by one. We'll start with planting which involves choosing the soil for your bonsai, learning the proper way to plant your bonsai, and learning how to re-pot as well. Planting is the first thing you will do on your bonsai growing journey. Later on, you need to re-pot your bonsai in order to remove excess roots to ensure the proper growth of your miniature tree.

Choosing the Best Soil for Your Bonsai

As mentioned earlier, there are certain types of soils and soil mixtures for bonsai trees. It's important to use the proper soil for growing your bonsai if you want to ensure its survival and if you want it to reach maturity. The soil to use must be able to supply your bonsai with all the nutrients it needs. It should also be able to drain well to allow for aeration while still being able to retain water to keep your bonsai hydrated. Most shops—whether online or physical—sell soils and soil mixtures meant for bonsai. But if you want to save some money, then you may also create your own soil mixture. Doing this also allows you to adjust the mixture to suit the type of bonsai you're planning to grow.

The quality of the soil you will use will have a direct impact on the vigor and health of your bonsai. Typically, bonsai trees that don't survive, or have poor health are those which grow in poor-quality soil. One common mistake beginners make, especially those who haven't done their research, is to use garden soil to grow their bonsai. Unfortunately, this type of soil tends to harden when it dries which, in turn, may harm your bonsai. To ensure the health of your bonsai, make sure that the soil mixture you use has these qualities:

- Aeration

The soil mixture you use must contain particles of the right size allowing air to pass between the particles. This allows oxygen to enter the roots. It also allows myocorrhizae and good bacteria to remain intact within the soil allowing the processing of food to occur before the root-hairs absorb them for photosynthesis.

- Drainage

After storing enough water to maintain proper moisture, the soil must be able to drain any excess water from the container immediately. Soils that lack this quality are water-retentive which may lead to an accumulation of salts. Also, when the soil retains too much water, this may result in root rot.

- Water retention

The soil you use must be able to absorb and retain adequate amounts of water. This helps maintain the proper levels of moisture for your bonsai in between watering sessions.

After checking to make sure that the soil you're planning to use has all of these qualities, the next thing you may want to know is whether you should use organic or inorganic soil. Soil mixtures are classified as either organic or inorganic. Organic soil mixtures contain dead plant matter like bark or leaf litter. However, the potential issues with these types of components is that over time, they will start breaking down which, in turn, reduces drainage. On the other hand, inorganic soil mixtures contain minimal to no organic components. Such mixtures absorb less water and nutrients, but they're more efficient at aeration and drainage. When choosing between these two classifications, consider what your plant needs.

Often, soil mixtures for bonsai trees contain common components. These components are added into the soil mixtures to help ensure the proper growth and health of bonsai trees. Therefore, when searching for the best soil mixture—or when planning to make your own—make sure the mixture contains the following:

- Akadama

This is a type of Japanese clay that has been hard-baked and is specifically made for bonsai growing. Before adding this component to your soil mixture, you must sift it first. It's also important to note that akadama may start breaking down after two years or so. This means that it may reduce the aeration of your soil to some extent. If you repot your bonsai regularly, this won't be an issue. Otherwise, you should combine this component with other components that allow for good drainage.

- Fine Grit or Gravel

This component can help the mixture with aeration and draining. You can also use it as the bottom layer of your bonsai container to improve drainage.

- Lava Rock

This is another component that retains water well. It also adds structure when you use it as part of your bonsai substrate. However, it's important to note that roots cannot grow into this component.

- Potting Compost (Organic)

This may include sand, peat moss, and perlite. Adding this to your bonsai soil mixture may work well. However, using potting compost on its own isn't recommended because it retains too much water and it doesn't drain or aerate well.

- Pumice

This is a soft type of volcanic product that absorbs nutrients and water relatively well. When using pumice in bonsai soil mixes, it can help with water retention while helping roots ramify well.

When it comes to soils and soil mixtures for bonsai, there is no standard type. This is because different types of bonsais require different types of soils and soil mixtures. Again, this is why it's important to learn all that you can about the specific type of bonsai you plan to grow. While knowing all the general information about bonsai soil can help, learning about the specific needs of the type of bonsai you plan to grow will ensure your success.

Generally, though, there are two main types of

mixtures for bonsai—one for coniferous bonsai trees and one for deciduous bonsai trees. Most coniferous or pine bonsai soil mixtures include 33% akadama, 33% lava rock, and 33% pumice. Most deciduous bonsai soil mixtures include 50% akadama, 25% lava rock, and 25% pumice.

Tips for Planting

While it's easy to appreciate the beauty of bonsai, getting to the point where you have a fully-grown miniature tree requires a lot of hard—and rewarding—work. You need to commit to the task while being disciplined, patient, and persistent when it comes to the actual growing process. To own a fully-grown bonsai, you have to go through years of growing, shaping, cultivation, and plant training. The good news is that the longer you stick with the journey of bonsai growing, the more rewarding it becomes. Here are some pointers to help guide you as you plant your bonsai:

1. Prepare your potting medium

After choosing the type of bonsai, deciding on the style you want your bonsai to have, and choosing the perfect container for it, the next thing you need to do is prepare the potting medium—in other words, the soil. We've already discussed how you can choose the best type of soil or soil mixture. With this knowledge (and the knowledge you've gathered through your research that is specific to the type of bonsai you have chosen), you can either purchase the soil mixture or make it using the appropriate components. When you have everything ready, follow these steps:

- Take your bonsai out of its nursery pot or container to expose the root ball.
- Cut off the bottom part of the root ball and remove about two-thirds of it.
- Use a rake to move the soil's surface until you've exposed the roots.
- Use a spray bottle to moisten the exposed roots.
- Remove any dead or unnecessary branches from your plant.
- Also, remove dead roots or any excess roots that might interfere when you place the plant in the pot.

2. Plant your bonsai

After preparing your young bonsai, it's time to plant. Here are some steps to guide you:

- Cut out a piece of wire screen following

the shape of the bottom of the container. Lay this inside the bottom of the container to prevent the soil from falling through the holes meant for drainage.

- Fill half of your pot with potting soil mixture.

- Carefully place your plant in the soil then fill the pot completely. Make sure to distribute the soil evenly around your plant.

3. Nourish your bonsai

After successfully planting your bonsai, it's time to nourish it. This involves watering your bonsai and adding fertilizer as needed. Later on, we will discuss the details of how to properly water and fertilize your bonsai. After this, all you have to do is wait for your bonsai to get used to its environment. Only when your bonsai has grown into a healthy, well-adapted plant can you start plant training.

Tips for Repotting

Repotting is an important part of bonsai growing, especially when the soil has already become hard and compact. When you keep your bonsai in a condition wherein it is slightly pot-bound, this helps slow down its growth while allowing it to mature. Doing this may also increase the production of flowers along with the aged appearance of the tree. Here are some signs that may indicate that your bonsai already needs repotting:

- A slower growth rate compared to the previous seasons.
- It becomes difficult to wet the soil.
- The water uptake of your bonsai decreases during summer.
- A rapid reduction in the size of your bonsai's leaves.
- The leaves of your bonsai fall off early during autumn.
- You notice a slight discoloration of your bonsai's foliage along with a decrease in gloss.
- Liverwort and algal slime start to form on the soil's surface.
- The root ball is rising slowly.
- The viability of your bonsai's leaves is decreasing.

Unless you notice these signs, the best possible time to repot your bonsai is during late winter and around mid-February. Then you can repot your bonsai again if you think there is a need to do so.

Since bonsai trees grow in small containers, they have limited space to absorb water and nutrients from the soil. The root systems of bonsais aren't able to expand as the root systems of trees in nature. Therefore, you need to ensure the proper soil proportion all the time and you can do this by repotting. As you repot your bonsai, this is also the perfect time to prune the old roots so that new roots can grow in their place.

For young bonsais, it's recommended to repot at least one time every year. For mature bonsais, you may repot them between two to five years. To determine when your mature bonsai already needs repotting, check its roots. If you're able to pull out your bonsai from its container easily with its root ball intact, this means that you can already repot your tree.

When it comes to repotting, you don't have to transfer your bonsai to a bigger pot or container. In fact, you don't even have to replace your bonsai's existing container. The main purpose of repotting is to simply replace the soil. However, there are certain types of bonsai trees which may require bigger containers for health and aesthetic purposes. Here are some steps for you to follow for repotting bonsai:

- Know when it's time to repot your bonsai

BONSAI

Be very careful when checking whether it's time to repot your bonsai or not. Lift your bonsai pot gently to check if the tree is pot-bound. If you think that it's time, you may try to gently pull out your bonsai. If it resists, it might not be time to repot yet. But if your bonsai comes out easily along with its root ball, then you know that it's time for repotting.

- Remove the old soil from the pot

It's essential to remove the old soil from the pot. In doing this, you will be removing the old soil from your bonsai's root system as well. Use a root hook for this purpose—you can use your fingers too. Also, remove any thick roots or those which have already grown heavily.

- Prune the roots

Pruning the roots makes your bonsai healthier. Just prune excess, old, thick, and long roots—not the ones which have small white hairs or those which are just growing. Before pruning, you may want to untangle the roots first so you can see which ones to prune and which ones to retain. It's also important to remove any sticky or blackish roots that show signs of rotting. Only prune less than 25% of the total root mass to ensure that your bonsai still have enough roots for the absorption of nutrients and water.

- Reposition your bonsai

Finally, return your bonsai to its pot. Reposition it carefully before adding soil. Then you can add the new soil to the pot all the way to the rim.

- More repotting tips

    o Don't repot your bonsai under the sun as this will dry up the roots quickly. Also, have a spray bottle on-hand for misting the roots to prevent dehydration.

    o Loosening up the roots by combing them carefully is essential as this makes it easier for you to prune.

    o Never remove all of the old soil from the roots of your bonsai. Retain some of the old soil which already contains good bacteria, enzymes, and the appropriate pH level for the new soil to adapt.

CHAPTER 6

PRUNING AND TRIMMING

The uniqueness of your bonsai will depend on how creative you are and how much you work on your plant. As your bonsai grows, there are certain things you must do to keep it healthy and to help it grow in the way you want it to. Two techniques that you will be doing with your bonsai frequently are pruning and trimming—and this is what this chapter is all about. While these techniques are similar to each other, trimming is simpler while pruning is a lot more elaborate.

Pruning is a process wherein you cut away any unnecessary growths on your bonsai. Often, you would have to prune leaves, buds, and branches. You also have to prune the roots of your bonsai, especially during repotting. Pruning is important because it helps control the development and growth of your bonsai. It helps you mold your tree into the style you've chosen so it will maintain that style even as it matures.

A bonsai tree is already considered mature enough for pruning the branches when it has established its trunk along with three branches. Another indication of the bonsai's maturity is when you have already seen its basic form. For branch pruning, you would have to remove existing limbs and emerging growths on your bonsai that don't coincide with the shape you want your bonsai to have. You may also prune apical buds and branch tips to hinder branch growth. Basically, you will prune anything that isn't harmonious or attractive to the overall appearance of your tree.

The pruning of branches is necessary for you to shape your bonsai, so it has a similar form to the same type of trees in the wild. This process helps your bonsai achieve the shape you desire in the following ways:

- The branches of a bonsai tree contributes to its shape. Pruning limbs helps provide light and space for the lateral buds and smaller branches to grow and develop.

- Pruning the branches also helps increase the overall size of the trunk. You would prune the trunk above a branch that you want to develop into a new trunk. This process of pruning also allows your bonsai to change direction as it grows.

Nevertheless, if your bonsai bears fruit or flowers, you must give it special consideration in terms of pruning because this process tends to inhibit the growth of fruits or flowers. Before you start pruning, you must first think about the needs of your tree and your own goals. That way, you won't end up compromising the health of your bonsai or the plans you have laid out for it.

Lateral buds refer to the limbs that emerge from the branches your bonsai already has. Over time, these buds will grow into new branches that you can train to be part of your plant's overall design. As you prune your bonsai, check all of the lateral buds as these will give you an idea about how they will grow in the future. Don't remove any lateral buds on the branches you prune that you believe will contribute to its overall form. If you notice an unnecessary branch that doesn't have lateral buds, you can prune it. Learning how to properly trim and prune your bonsai is essential if you want to successfully achieve your bonsai growing goals. With that being said, let's go through these techniques one at a time.

How to Properly Prune Your Bonsai

To achieve the look you desire for your bonsai, you need to prune it frequently, consistently, and properly. There are two main types of pruning you can perform on your bonsai depending on your purpose:

1. Pruning for aesthetic purposes

If you want to prune your tree for the purpose of aesthetics, the best time to do this is when your bonsai is dormant. This ensures that you don't stunt the growth of your tree and you won't end up damaging it. Most trees are dormant during the winter season, so you may start pruning between the months of November to February.

For this type of pruning, remove any big branches

protruding from your bonsai. Also, remove any branches that have an undesirable appearance or those which have unnatural and unharmonious twists. To remove these branches, cut them right above a node. Make sure that when you're pruning the branches, you still maintain its balanced look. If you want to keep the neat appearance of your bonsai, the best tool to use is a branch cutter.

In some cases, you want more light to pass through the canopy of your bonsai so the lower branches can gain access to light as well. For this purpose, prune some of the branches and twigs at the top of your bonsai. Doing this also allows you to shape your tree's canopy as needed. Again, use branch cutters for this so as to maintain the shape and balance of the canopy. If, while you're pruning, you discover small offshoots—called suckers—you can pluck these off gently to maintain the aesthetic appeal of your bonsai.

2. Pruning for maintenance purposes

This type of pruning is more important, and you should do it regularly to keep your tree happy and healthy. When pruning for the purpose of maintenance, here are some tips to keep in mind:

- o Remove all dead leaves, wood, and weeds from your bonsai and from its pot. When removing weeds, be very careful so you don't end up damaging the roots of your plant.

- If you find any crossed or broken branches, remove these too. When branches cross, this might result in wounds that allow pests or diseases to infect your bonsai. The same thing goes for branches that are broken, which is why you should remove these too.

- For each of the branches of your bonsai, they should only have a maximum of four nodes each. Nodes refer to the joints where leaves grow. Use branch cutters to prune excess nodes from the branches.

- Pruning for maintenance must be done during the active period of trees—usually the spring and summer seasons.

Pruning is an essential aspect of growing bonsai, both for aesthetic and health purposes. If you know how to perform this method correctly, you won't have to worry about harming your bonsai. To do this, you must also learn how to properly prune the different parts of your bonsai:

- Pruning the branches of your bonsai

When your tree is mature enough to allow for branch pruning, you can start planning which branches to cut. For this task, it's recommended to use pruning shears or a concave branch cutter. Make sure that your tool is sharp so you can make quick, clean cuts. After making a cut, seal it with a special bonsai sealant, glue or paste for quicker healing.

Prune branches that are rotten, broken, and those that don't contribute to the overall aesthetic of your bonsai. This includes oversized branches and those growing in odd directions. You may also prune any branches which are growing well but don't fit into the plans you have made for the shape and style of your bonsai. Removing these imperfections gives your bonsai a better look and feel.

While your bonsai is still young, pruning its branches shouldn't be your priority. At this stage, you should only focus on pruning the roots, the nebari, and the trunk of your tree. Also, you shouldn't prune your bonsai during extreme temperatures or weather. Doing this might cause undue stress and damage to your bonsai.

When it comes to branch pruning, it's also important to consider the type of bonsai you're growing. This helps you determine the best time to prune. Generally, it's recommended to prune the branches of deciduous trees during spring, while it's recommended to prune the branches of coniferous trees between autumn and winter. Either way, don't prune your bonsai when it's too cold.

- Pruning the buds of your bonsai

Typically, you would prune the buds of your bonsai at the same time when you perform branch pruning. Also, you should only do bud pruning on a mature tree. As with branch pruning, bud pruning aims to bring balance and harmony to your bonsai's final form. Before you start, you should know the benefits of this process.

Sometimes, pruning buds is more beneficial than pruning branches, especially when your bonsai has achieved its completed form. Bud pruning allows you to maintain this completed form without promoting extra growth. This type of pruning is also recommended for the suppression of branch growth without having to prune the branches.

For deciduous trees, bud pruning helps maintain the beauty of the tree, especially if your bonsai has lush foliage and attractive branches. For coniferous trees, bud pruning is more preferred instead of leaf pruning. The reason for this is that for these types of trees, leaf pruning might have an effect on the quality of leaves that grow after and it might even cause damage to your bonsai. In some cases, bud pruning is essential, especially if your bonsai has lateral buds that aren't showing growth. Bud pruning helps save the branches with this condition.

The best time to prune buds is when they're growing on your bonsai's trunk. Usually, this happens during the spring season, but for some trees, this may happen until autumn. Therefore, you need to monitor the buds of your bonsai and prune them as needed. However, if your bonsai isn't healthy or it's in a weakened state—such as after you have repotted it—you shouldn't perform bud pruning. Also, bud pruning isn't recommended when the trunk of your bonsai is still in the process of thickening.

In order to prune buds, you would have to pinch them with your fingers or prune them using scissors. As soon as undesirable buds emerge, prune them. There are certain buds called "apical buds" that encourage branch growth. Therefore, pruning these slows down the growth of the branches to control your tree's overall size. You must first perform bud pruning on the older branches of your bonsai located at the top. Of course, you should also make sure to water and fertilize your bonsai before and after bud pruning. This helps your bonsai recover from pruning.

- Pruning the leaves of your bonsai

Before you start pruning the leaves of your bonsai, think about your purpose for doing so—both your short-term and long-term goals. You can do leaf pruning on a mature bonsai for the refinement of its shape and length. Leaf pruning involves pruning the parts of your bonsai which are already well-developed.

You can maintain the vibrancy and health of your bonsai by finding leaves growing in pairs. Then as you prune your bonsai, simply remove one leaf from each of these pairs. If your bonsai already has a desirable appearance and form but its leaves have become too dense, you can cut them in half. This allows light to pass through to the inner part of your tree and it also improves ventilation. If you have pruned a lot of leaves from your bonsai, it's recommended to place it in a shaded but bright area for about ten days to help it recover.

After pruning, it's important to cover cuts and wounds with paste, glue or sealant. This prevents the leaking of sap and it also helps with the healing of your bonsai. Also, it's recommended to water your bonsai right after pruning to moisten the soil fully. These steps are necessary to help your tree heal after you've pruned its parts.

Clever Trimming Techniques

Before you start trimming your bonsai, you must first determine the best time to do so. Trimming at the proper time allows your bonsai to heal adequately before the seasons change and the weather gets too extreme. When it comes to trimming, the ideal time varies between species. But for most types of trees, the perfect time is between spring and summer seasons. You can actually ask this—and other important questions about your bonsai—from the shop where you purchased your seed or starter tree.

Keep in mind that pruning and trimming leave open wounds which may potentially cause an infection in your plant. This is why it's important to use some type of glue or sealant to prevent this from happening. Since bonsais require regular pruning and trimming to maintain their health and shape, you may want to come up with a schedule which gives your tree enough time to heal between each pruning or trimming session.

Trimming the branches of your bonsai helps control their growth and direction. You would do this for aesthetic purposes and to maintain your tree's structural stability. To maintain the aesthetic appeal of your tree, remove the branches that cloud or clutter its artistic line. These may include branches that grow at sharp angles, those that cross one another, and branches that grow across the trunk of your bonsai. To maintain structural stability, avoid trimming branches that may increase the growth in weaker parts of your tree. But if you notice that your bonsai's trunk is leaning too heavily towards one direction, you may trim a few branches to preserve balance. Here are some clever tips and guidelines when it comes to trimming branches:

- Remove the branches known as "yagome" which grow at the bottom of your bonsai. Such branches tend to absorb all of the nutrients which, in turn, may hinder the growth of other branches.

- Remove the branches known as "kan-nuki eda" which grow on both sides of your bonsai and have the same height. Remove one of these branches on either of the sides.

- Remove branches known as "dou-nuki eda" which grow from the center of the trunk as these tend to hinder a good condition of growth.

- Remove any branches which cross the trunk.

- Remove branches known as "kousa eda" which cross with other branches.

- Remove any branches that grow close to one another, have the same length, and grow in the same direction. These branches cause disruptions to the overall form of your bonsai.

- Remove branches known as "sagari eda"

which grow straight in a downward direction.

- Remove branches known as "tachi eda" which grow straight in an upward direction.

- Remove branches known as "kuruma eda" which grow in a single spot but in several directions.

- Remove branches known as "gyaku eda" which grow in the opposite direction of the main branch they grow from.

- Remove branches known as "Tochoshi" which grows significantly longer compared to the other branches. That is unless you need such a branch to adjust how other branches are growing.

Finally, you should also trim the roots of your bonsai. Do this to maintain a relative proportion of the parts of your bonsai which are underground and those which are above ground. Trimming the root system occasionally prevents it from growing at a very fast rate. If the root system of your bonsai grows too rapidly, you would have to prune it more frequently which, in turn, increases the risk of root rot or infections.

CHAPTER 7

WATERING AND FERTILIZING

Previously, we mentioned that there is a certain way to water bonsai. Since this is a special type of plant, it requires special methods and techniques to help it grow and flourish. In most cases, you must water your bonsai twice, and there is a reason for this. As long as you have chosen the correct type of soil or soil mixture for your bonsai, you won't have to worry about overwatering it.

There are several reasons why it's recommended to water bonsai twice. For one, you would be flushing the dust from the soil so the root zone can access fresh air. Another reason is for cooling the pot and the roots of your bonsai. Also, watering twice softens any fertilizer cakes or to reactivate fertilizer salts. Finally, doing this ensures that the entire root zone gets wet. You can think of it this way—the purpose of watering your bonsai the first time is to "prime the soil." The second time is when you actually water and fertilize your plant because the soil has already been prepared.

If you have decided to use organic fertilizers, the first pass at watering moistens the soil and the fertilizer salts thus, reactivating them. If you have decided to use a liquid type of inorganic fertilizer, then you should apply it during your second pass at watering when the soil is ready to absorb it. After that, the soil can start distributing the fertilizer to the roots and to the rest of your bonsai.

If you have decided to use organic fertilizer, the same thing happens. The first time you water your bonsai, you are also priming its soil. This also loosens the fertilizer particles which are already mixed in with the soil. During this first pass, you would also soften the fertilizer cakes that you have placed on the surface of the soil. The second time you water your bonsai, this is when different processes start happening. You'll notice the fertilizer cakes breaking up and getting washed into the soil. After that, the soil can start absorbing the fertilizer and distributing it to the roots and to the rest of your bonsai.

Apart from watering your bonsai, fertilizing it is also important. Fertilizing your bonsai provides it with the essential macronutrients—nitrogen, phosphorus, and potassium—along with essential micronutrients to support its growth and development. These nutrients can also help your bonsai combat diseases and pests that might compromise the health of your plant.

Another important reason why you should fertilize your bonsai, especially during autumn is to help it withstand the winter season. Fertilizing your bonsai during this season also allows it to store energy in its different parts so that when spring comes, your plant can emerge from its dormant state strong and healthy. The energy stored by your bonsai is what it will use to open new buds and produce new leaves. If you want your bonsai to be strong enough to push itself out of dormancy come spring, autumn fertilization is essential. Then you should continue fertilizing your bonsai throughout the other season in order to replenish the energy it has lost from pushing out of its dormant state.

Proper Ways of Watering Bonsai Plants

One of the most important parts of cultivating and growing a bonsai is watering it properly. This promotes its growth and development. The fact is, bonsais can die when they get dehydrated. Therefore, watering your tree correctly is key to its health and survival. There are several methods, tips, and even misconceptions about surrounding this particular topic. But as long as you learn all the correct information, you can properly water your bonsai each and every time. Let's break down the different topics that are part of watering bonsai plants:

The factors that affect the water requirements of bonsais

How frequent you would water your bonsai depends on a number of factors. These factors help you determine the frequency of watering your bonsai since they affect the water requirements and drying time of bonsais. These factors are:

- The soil mixture of your bonsai

When it comes to soil mixtures, the components that store water are clay, peat moss, vermiculite, and fines (both organic and inorganic). If your soil mixture contains high amounts of these components, these decrease the ability of the soil mixture to drain water thus, increasing the capacity for water retention. In such a case, you would have to wait for longer periods of time between watering sessions. But you shouldn't increase the volume of water over 25% as this might decrease aeration and cause root rot. Conversely, if the soil mixture you have chosen drains water well, then you may have to water your bonsai more frequently.

- The size of the pot

The bigger your bonsai's pot is, the longer it would take for the soil to dry up. This type of pot is ideal for fast-growing and water-thirsty types of bonsai, so you won't have to water them frequently.

- The size of your plant

The bigger your plant is, the more leaves it would have. In such a case, the soil may dry out more rapidly compared to when you have a smaller plant with fewer leaves. When you notice that the soil dries out quickly, this is an indication that you must water your bonsai frequently. In fact, you should avoid the soil from drying out as this might cause your bonsai to be dehydrated. If you're growing a bonsai outdoors, it's best to have a one-day interval between watering sessions. This schedule is easy to remember and it's ideal because it prevents the occurrence of root rot.

- The type of fertilizer you use

Some types of fertilizer tend to increase the drying time of soil which, in turn, affects the growth rate of the bonsai tree. These fertilizers accelerate the decomposition of the organic part of the soil thus causing it to collapse prematurely. If you use these types of fertilizer, you would have to increase the frequency of watering to prevent the soil from drying up.

- Plant diseases

If you notice that your bonsai suffers from root rot or other root problems, you must stop watering it for some time. Allow your plant to dry out so the diseases don't become worse. On the other hand, if you notice that your bonsai is starting to dry up or wilt, then you should start watering it more.

- Environmental factors

When there are strong winds, this increases the transpiration of your bonsai and if this happens, you should decrease the watering intervals of your bonsai. Generally, though, you should keep your bonsai away from the wind as this might have an adverse effect on your bonsai's growth, development, and health.

Most types of bonsai require a lot of sunlight in order to thrive. But if your bonsai is under direct sunlight, this increases evaporation and transpiration. This means that you have to water your bonsai more frequently as well. Other factors which increase transpiration and the drying out of the soil are high temperature and humidity. This may happen even when your plant isn't exposed to sunlight. In such a case, you would have to reduce the intervals between your bonsai's watering sessions.

The best time to water bonsais

The best time to water your bonsai is when its soil feels a little dry. Although there aren't any rules about the best time to water bonsai, you may want to avoid watering your tree in the afternoon and using cold water. The reason for this is that sunlight warmed the soil up already and when you water your bonsai at this time, it will cool down rapidly. Also, you don't have to water your bonsai when its soil still feels wet. One thing you must avoid completely is for the soil and your bonsai to dry out completely. The longer you care for your bonsai, the better you will get at determining when it's time for a watering session.

Checking the moisture of the soil

The easiest and most accurate way to determine whether it's time to water your bonsai or not is by checking the moisture of the soil. There are a few methods you can use for this task including:

BONSAI

- Use a **soil moisture meter** which measures the root level moisture of the soil.

- Use the **finger method** where you would stick your finger about an inch deep into the soil to check whether it's moist or not.

- Use the **chopstick method** where you insert a plain wooden chopstick about an inch or two deep into the soil, leave it there for up to 10 minutes, and pull it up to check if the color of the chopstick changed.

Watering methods for bonsai trees

There are also different methods you can use for watering your bonsai. The method we explained in the introduction of this chapter is the simplest and most common way to water your bonsai. Other methods include:

- **Natural watering** wherein you simulate rainfall. For this method, you would soak the soil of your bonsai until excess water starts running out of the pot's drainage holes. Perform the soaking for up to 20 minutes and wait until all excess water drains out. As for the foliage of your bonsai, you can use a spray bottle for misting.

- Using **water hoses** and **watering cans** is

also a common practice. However, you must be careful with this method because when you water using a single stream of water that is overly concentrated, this tends to wash out the soil. Therefore, when using a watering can, fit it with a fine rose. For a water hose, turn it on a mist or low-pressure setting before watering.

- Use an automatic **drip irrigation system** for when you don't have the time to water your plants. However, you should still check on the moisture level of your plant's soil regularly.

- Use **large collections** such as **automatic irrigation systems** or **overhead sprinklers** when you're caring for several bonsais and you don't want to water them one at a time.

- Use **immersion** or **dunking** for bonsais which have dried out completely. This method is a "quick fix," but it's not always recommended. Doing this frequently might damage the roots of your bonsai.

More watering tips to keep in mind

To add to your knowledge of watering bonsai properly, here are some final tips for you:

- It's not always necessary to water your bonsai daily—it's better to check your tree and its soil first.

- Use plain tap water for watering your bonsai. You may also use rainwater once in a while to eliminate any salt that has accumulated in the soil or the pot.

- When using a water hose for the task, make sure that it hasn't been laying under the sun as the water that comes out from it will be either warm or hot.

- When watering a bonsai with flowers, be careful not to hit them.

Do Bonsai Plants Need Fertilizer?

Fertilizing your bonsai regularly is important, especially during the growing season for the survival of your bonsai. Normally, when trees grow in nature, their root systems extend while searching for nutrients in the soil. Since bonsai grow in small containers, there is a need to fertilize them to maintain the nutrient content of the soil. The main components of plant fertilizers are nitrogen, phosphorus, and potassium which appear on labels as NPK. Each of these macronutrients has its own purposes for the growth and development of the plant.

Nitrogen helps increase the growth of stems and leaves, phosphorus helps encourage the healthy growth of the roots, flowers, and fruit, and potassium helps maintain the overall health of the plant. Different fertilizer products have their own NPK and the ratio you would choose depends on the type of bonsai you're growing. Also, fertilizers contain other nutrients aside from these three basic components. All of these components work together to keep the plant strong, healthy, and thriving.

For most types of bonsai, the best time to apply fertilizer is throughout the whole growing season. Once your tree has reached maturity, you can reduce the frequency of applying fertilizer. Of course, this also depends on a number of factors including the tree's health, the time of the year, and the bonsai's current developmental stage. All throughout the growing season, you should feed your bonsai with fertilizer every week. Come late summer and early autumn, the nutrient absorption rate of your bonsai may decrease which, in turn, also causes the growth rate to slow down. During this time, you can reduce the frequency of fertilization to once a month. Here are some fertilizing strategies for you depending on the type of bonsai:

- When fertilizing **deciduous trees**, do so

weekly throughout the growing season. As soon as the leaves of the tree have fallen off, you should stop applying fertilizer. During autumn and winter, you can feed your tree a 0-10-0 fertilizer.

- When fertilizing **conifer trees**, do so weekly throughout the growing season. Come winter, you must still continue fertilizing your tree at least a couple of times. During autumn and winter, you can feed your tree a 0-10-0 fertilizer.

- When fertilizing **sub-tropical** and **tropical trees**, do so weekly throughout the growing season. These types of trees continue growing all year; therefore, you should feed them every month no matter what the season is.

It's never a good idea to starve your tree. Fertilizing it regularly helps maintain its size while preventing it from growing spindly, unattractive limbs. However, if your bonsai gets sick, allow it to recover first before you continue feeding it with fertilizer. When it comes to fertilizing bonsai, the general rule is to only feed healthy trees.

When feeding your bonsai with fertilizer, read the directions on the product's packaging carefully. This allows you to use the proper quantities of fertilizer as well as the frequency of feeding. If your bonsai has passed through the training stage, you may slightly reduce the quantity of fertilizer you use. This helps balance the growth of the tree rather than stimulating it. When you use solid fertilizer, you may want to use a fertilizer cover as well. This ensures that the fertilizer stays where it's supposed to.

Although there is very little risk of overwatering your bonsai—especially if you have chosen the proper pot and soil mixture—there is such a thing as overfeeding a bonsai. Be very careful with this because it might cause serious adverse consequences to the health of your tree. Here are some steps to guide you when it comes to fertilizing your bonsai:

- Decide whether you want to use a granulated or liquid fertilizer. For granulated fertilizer, you would have to dissolve it in water first or simply place it in the soil for a time-release feeding. For liquid fertilizer, all you have to do is add it to the water and feed it to your bonsai.

- Before feeding your bonsai, read the instructions on the label on how to apply it.

- Remember to fertilize your young bonsai throughout the entire growing season. For bonsais in refinement, you can start feeding fertilizer after the spring growth has matured or hardened off already.

- You may want to create a fertilizing schedule for your bonsai to make it easier for you to remember. Remember that the health of your plant depends on how you take care of it. And since fertilizing is an important aspect of growing bonsai, having a schedule will really help out.

- After you have fertilized your plant, you should also check the progress of its growth. Do this after one or two days so you can see if any changes have happened.

CHAPTER 8

WIRING TECHNIQUES AND CLAMPING

Wiring and clamping are techniques used in bonsai training. Wiring gives you control over the growth of your bonsai. You would use wires to shape the branches and trunk of your tree, so they will grow to the shape you desire. As soon as your bonsai has an established root system, you can begin this process. Wiring isn't a one-time thing—it's a continuous process that you would have to do stage by stage depending on how you want your bonsai to grow into maturity.

Wiring is essential for shaping your bonsai because these miniature trees don't grow into the forms we desire naturally. Through the process of wiring, you can guide the growth of the tree allowing it to grow in unnatural—but visually appealing—forms. To simply put it, wiring is done to contribute to the

BONSAI

aesthetics of a bonsai tree. Through wiring, you can form your bonsai artistically to show off your own style and personality.

The types of wire used for bonsai wiring are either aluminum or copper wire. For this task, choose a wire that is approximately a third of the trunk's or branch's diameter. Aluminum wire is recommended for beginners because it's easier to manipulate. It's more flexible than copper, but it's not as sturdy. If you decide to use aluminum wire, you must monitor the trunk or branches that you have wired every two weeks. On the other hand, copper wire is sturdier and harder. This means that it's able to hold its form for a longer time without getting detached or displaced. However, copper wire may end up causing damage to your bonsai's trunk or branches if you don't monitor it carefully. When left unchecked and unattended, this type of wire might cut or bruise parts of your plant. Therefore, you must monitor the condition and growth of your bonsai regularly after wiring.

To achieve the form you desire for your bonsai, it's best to start wiring while your plant is young and healthy. The best time to start wiring is after repotting as this will help support the new growth. The perfect time for wiring also depends on the type of bonsai you're growing. For instance, proper timing differs between deciduous and coniferous trees:

- The best time to wire **deciduous trees** is during the early part of the spring season. Do this when new buds are starting to develop on your bonsai's limbs. This is the perfect time for wiring as it provides an ideal appearance of the branches and trunk of your bonsai before new growth and leaves start developing. This means that you can clearly see the limbs which, in turn, allows you to apply the wire without distractions.

- The best time to wire **coniferous trees** is between late autumn and early winter. The reason for this is that the foliage of these types of bonsai trees renew every year. This means that the limbs will always have foliage no matter the time of the year. You can start wiring when the sap is at the lowest part of the branches. This makes them more flexible and easier to wire.

One thing to remember is that you shouldn't wire your bonsai if it's suffering from a disease or any other kind of condition. Also, check the strength of the branches before wiring as weak branches might break when you apply wire to them. Make sure your plant is strong and healthy first, especially the parts you plan to wire. That way, you won't end up damaging your tree in the process.

Various Wiring Techniques to Try

Wiring is a process that's crucial for bonsai training and styling. This involves wrapping wire around the trunk or branches of your miniature tree. This allows you to bend, reposition, and style your bonsai to achieve the final form you want it to have when it matures. Wiring isn't an easy or fast process. In fact, it may take a couple of months before the wired parts of your bonsai will be permanently set. Only then can you remove the wire carefully.

There are a lot of things involved in wiring—it's a very tricky process to learn. The two main wiring techniques are double-wiring which involves wiring two branches adjacent to each other and having the same thickness to each other and single-wiring which involves wiring branches one at a time. Wire all of the branches that you want to shape before you start bending them. Start wiring branches from the trunk of your bonsai to the main branches, then the tree's secondary branches. Make sure that the wire you use is thick enough to support the trunk or branches you want to bend and shape. Now, let's go through these main wiring techniques step by step:

- Double-wiring

- Choose two branches adjacent to each other and with the same thickness.

- Make an estimation of the length of wire you need for the task.

- Before wiring these branches, wrap the wire around your bonsai's trunk twice so it doesn't move around.

- Continue by wiring the base of the first branch all the way to the tip. Then you can start wiring the second branch.

- Make sure to wrap the wire at a 45-degree angle as this allows the wire to promote the thickening of the tree while it follows the new shape.

- **Single-wiring**

    - Make an estimation of the length of wire you need for the task.

    - Wrap the wire around the trunk twice first before you start wiring branches one at a time at a 45-degree angle.

    - If you plan to wire several branches in one area, make sure to arrange the wires neatly.

After wrapping the trunk and branches with wire, it's time to start bending them. Be careful when bending and repositioning so you don't break or damage the trunk or any of the branches of your bonsai. Gently grip the outer part of the branch and bend from the inside. This method ensures that you won't split or break the branches. Bending should be done in a singular motion—repeated bending may damage the branches. Also, you may want to step back after bending each of the branches to check the overall look of your bonsai to ensure that you're getting the look you planned to achieve.

Wire Anchoring

When wiring branches, you would have to wrap the wire at a certain angle—usually 45-degrees—around the branches. Before this, you should secure the wire first, so it doesn't move around when you start bending the branches. This is very important because when the wire starts twisting around as you bend your bonsai's branches, this causes damage, especially to the bark. The process of wire anchoring can help prevent this. There are different methods of wire anchoring you can do depending on the part of the bonsai:

- Wire anchoring for the trunk

When wiring the trunk of your bonsai, you can anchor the wire into its growing medium. To do this, insert a significant length of the wire into the soil. Make sure that the anchored wire is adjacent to the trunk, it's coiled around the trunk twice, and there aren't any gaps.

- Wire anchoring for the branches

When wiring the branches of your bonsai, anchor the wire by wrapping it around the trunk at least two times.

- Wire anchoring for branch forks

Loop the wire over the branch forks first before you start wrapping the wire around the branches. Position the loop over the branch fork if you plan to bend the branches upward. Position the loop below the branch fork if you plan to bend the branches downward.

Gaps and Spacing

Wiring is a process that involves both hands. You should hold the branches gently but firmly with one hand while using your other hand to apply the wire. Make sure that the wire you wrap around the branches is firmly pressed and in full contact with them. Otherwise, you will end up with gaps.

Basically, gaps are the areas where the wire isn't in contact with the trunk or branches. Gaps shouldn't exist for one very important reason. When it's time to start bending the branches and there are some branches which you need to "overbend" in order to get the form or position you desire, having gaps increases the risk of the branch breaking or snapping.

The Dangers of Wire Bite

Although wiring is an important part of bonsai growing, it does come with one very dangerous condition known as wire bite. As you wire the trunk or branches of your bonsai, you would be breaking them little by little. Over time, these small breaks heal as the wired parts of your bonsai set in their positions.

But if you don't wire correctly or you don't wire at the proper time, your bonsai might suffer from wire bite. Wiring a deciduous tree during early spring—when it hasn't pushed new growth yet—can cause wire bite after a few weeks. This occurs when the wired branches start thickening but aren't able to do so because of the wire. In such a situation, the branch starts swelling between the wire. If left unchecked, the branch might even end up swallowing the wire! You want to prevent this from happening as it may cause scars on the trunk or branches of your tree which will affect its aesthetic appeal.

Removing the Wire

After wiring, you must regularly check and observe your bonsai to see if you can already remove the wire.

Usually, it would take a few weeks for the position or form to set before you can remove the wire. Do this carefully using the proper tools, so you don't damage your bonsai's trunk or branches. The best tool to use is a wire cutter that's specifically made and designed for bonsai growing.

What Does Clamping Mean in Bonsai Growing?

Clamping is another bonsai training technique, though it's not as common as wiring. You would perform clamping as part of shaping and styling your bonsai. Much like wiring, you may use clamping to change the growing direction of your bonsai's trunk or branches. Just make sure that when you perform this technique, you do it carefully and correctly so that the clamp won't damage your tree or create an unintended effect.

It's important to note that changing the growing direction of a bonsai's trunk or branches isn't required. But if you see your bonsai as a piece of art, then clamping can be a fun activity for you. After you have attached the clamp to your bonsai, leave it in position for some time. Over time, you can start tightening the clamp bit by bit in order to force the trunk or branches to grow in a certain direction. You may also move the position of the clamp to promote continuous growth in the right direction.

BONSAI

When it comes to clamping, one thing you shouldn't forget is that you should never make forceful movements with the tool. Instead, simply apply gentle pressure on your tree. This ensures that the circulation of your bonsai doesn't get cut off which, in turn, might end up killing your tree. If this is your first time to perform clamping, use the lightest setting first. Then as soon as you see some movement or a change in direction, you can start tightening the clamp little by little.

As with wiring, clamping is a slow process that requires patience and careful observation. Combining clamping and wiring allows you to change the growing direction of your bonsai's trunk and its branches too. But you only have to do this if you want to see a huge change in how your bonsai is growing. The length of time you would keep the clamp on your bonsai depends on how much of a change you want to make. There are some cases where people leave the clamps in place for a number of years!

Also, the type of clamp to use depends on the type of bend you want your bonsai to acquire. Even though all clamps possess bumper ends as a safety feature to not cause damage, there are several shapes and sizes available. This variation allows you to work on your bonsai tree no matter what size it is. Some clamps are even designed to be used alongside wiring techniques.

You can also use clamps to straighten the trunk or branches of your bonsai. At the end of the day, it all depends on what you're trying to achieve through clamping.

CHAPTER 9

DEFOLIATION AND DEADWOOD TECHNIQUES

Most beginners deal with the same issue—being able to maintain the health of their bonsai. This is especially true for those who don't educate themselves enough before they start the process. For a lot of people, they believe that growing a bonsai is basically the same as growing any other kinds of plants. Of course, this isn't true. If you want to maintain a healthy bonsai, you should know how to take care of it properly.

Adding the aesthetic value of your tree involves allowing it to grow in a small, proportionate container with the appropriate type of soil. Growing and cultivating bonsai requires a lot of care and a broad knowledge of the different methods and techniques used specifically for bonsai. In this article, we will be focusing on defoliation and deadwood techniques which are also an important part of the whole process.

Defoliation is a crucial process though not all types of plants can adopt it. Nevertheless, defoliation allows the dwarfing of foliage to some types of deciduous trees. On the other hand, deadwood techniques are typically applied to the branches of coniferous trees. While deciduous trees shed their branches regularly and the wounds left are able to heal after some time, coniferous trees retain their dead limbs. After some time, these limbs start getting eroded and weathered. You may remove these limbs completely or partially though this might end up causing damage to your tree's shape or its aged appearance. If you want to retain these limbs, you must treat them chemically for their preservation and give them the proper coloration. Also, you need to shape the deadwood so that it fits into your aesthetic plan.

How to Defoliate Your Bonsai Plant

Defoliating bonsai is a process wherein you cut all of the leaves when the summer season comes along. This process forces your bonsai to grow new leaves; therefore, increasing ramification and decreasing the leaf size. You should only perform defoliation if you're growing a deciduous type of bonsai tree. Also, you should only perform it if you know that your tree is healthy enough to survive defoliation—a very demanding process. When it comes to defoliation, you don't have to do this on the entire tree. You may only defoliate parts of it for the purpose of restoring balance in your bonsai.

Defoliation is an important technique for the aesthetic growth of your bonsai. It promotes the goal of growing bonsai——to create aesthetic pleasure, balance, and harmony. The main purpose of defoliation is the reduction of the size of your bonsai's leaves. Over time, this process may increase the number of leaves and stimulate growth as well. Another benefit of defoliation is that it can help stimulate the development of branchlets which, in turn, allows double the growth in one growing season.

If you have a deciduous type of bonsai tree, then you may consider defoliating it. But before you do, make sure that your tree is growing vigorously and is at the peak of health. The leaves of plants—including bonsai—help them grow. Photosynthesis happens in the leaves; therefore, if you start removing the leaves of a sick or an infected bonsai, this will make the condition worse. Although defoliation can be beneficial to your bonsai, it poses two major risks as well. First, it will shock your bonsai's system. Second, it will restrict your bonsai's ability to grow. So, if you have an unhealthy tree, defoliation might end up killing it.

Observe all aspects of your bonsai before making the decision to defoliate. If you see any weak branches, it's best to delay this process as it might weaken those branches further. Give them time to grow leaves, buds, and grow stronger too. If this is your first time to defoliate your bonsai, you should only defoliate a third of the whole tree until you gain more confidence and experience.

Although you may pinch off some buds and leaves using your fingers, the best type of tool for defoliation is a sharp pair of pruning scissors. This ensures that you can make clean cuts which will heal quickly and properly. To ensure the cleanliness of your pruning scissors, make sure to wipe them clean before and after each defoliation session. This also prevents the transmission of bacteria to the cuts and wounds.

The best month to perform defoliation is June. This gives ample time to your bonsai for growing new leaves in preparation for winter. Also, it's best to start defoliation after the new growths that emerged during the spring season has already hardened off. It's never a good idea to defoliate your bonsai when it's dormant. Instead, do this during the season when your bonsai is growing leaves actively. Here are the types of defoliation you can perform on bonsais:

- Partial

This type of defoliation won't cause as much of a shock to your bonsai's system compared to complete defoliation. One reason for this is that the trauma felt by the bonsai gets spread out over the whole growing season. Another reason is that you would only remove a portion of the leaves. This means that a lot of smaller leaves will remain—and these will continue performing photosynthesis. Here are the steps to follow for partial defoliation:

  - First, remove the biggest leaves—these typically grow at the tips of the branches. Removing these leaves gives space for light to pass through your bonsai to the lower and center parts thus stimulating vigorous growth.

  - Continue defoliating by removing the rest of the large leaves. Over time, these will be replaced by smaller leaves.

It's as simple as that! After you've partially defoliated your bonsai, place it somewhere with a lot of sun. Also, give your bonsai a lot of water for it to recover faster. This type of defoliation is recommended for beginner bonsai growers. This is because there's a very low likelihood that you will make a mistake that would adversely affect the health and shape of your bonsai.

- Complete

You may only attempt complete defoliation after you've gained more experience with partial defoliation. As the name suggests, this involves removing all the leaves of your bonsai. Only do this after the new leaves have completely hardened off—this means that they have a dark green color and they have already become tough and shiny. Here are the steps to follow for partial defoliation:

    o Remove each of the leaves at their base while making sure that you've left the petioles (stems). As new buds emerge, these petioles will dry up and start falling off.

    o Continue doing this until you've removed all the leaves of your bonsai. Once all of the leaves have been removed, it becomes easier for you to see your bonsai's overall structure.

After this process, place your bonsai in a place where it can get some—but not a lot—of sun. Also, your bonsai won't need a lot of water because there won't be any leaves left to feed. After a few weeks, new buds will start emerging. The leaves that grow from these buds will be significantly smaller since they would have less time to develop during the growing season.

Deadwood Techniques for Bonsai

Deadwood techniques for bonsai are performed for aesthetic and practical purposes. Dead wood can appear on bonsai which have encountered disease. As a bonsai grower, you have the choice to allow this dead wood to stay on your tree or you can remove it too. But as aforementioned, the removal of dead wood might cause harm to the aged illusion you want your bonsai to have. Doing this might also compromise the overall shape of your bonsai. This is actually why most bonsai growers leave dead wood alone. If you're one such person, you must have the dead wood on your bonsai treated. This ensures the preservation of the coloration of the dead wood. It's also important for you to do everything you can to prevent pests from harming your plant. Then, you should also shape the dead wood to fit into your aesthetic plans for your tree.

Deadwood techniques are essential, especially in terms of aesthetics. Seasoned bonsai growers know how to perform these techniques. But even as a beginner, you can learn these techniques to prepare yourself for when you need to start doing them on your own. Here are some benefits of performing deadwood techniques:

- To conceal the defects of your bonsai such as oversized parts or misplaced branches.

- It helps give your bonsai an illusion of being old.

- To disguise your bonsai's trunk after you have reduced it because it has grown excessively.

- To highlight the overall appearance of your bonsai.

Different deadwood techniques can be applied to different plants. To help you understand these techniques better, here are some things you should know:

- Driftwood and Shari

The driftwood style applies to bonsais that have a large dead trunk holding dead branches. This style is also known as "sharamiki." You can carve the dead wood of the bonsai according to the shape that you want. In the end, it should look like the remains of a tree beaten by the weather.

Shari are usually found on a bonsai's main trunk. A small shari runs vertically or near the front of the trunk. Shari aren't very common because bonsai enthusiasts don't see them as having a lot of aesthetic value. Usually, living bark surrounds shari or it can be concealed by growing branches. The main factors that cause the formation of shari are lightning damage, failing branches or trunk damage.

- Jin

This deadwood technique can be used on the branches of your bonsai. You can also use it at the top of your plant. The aim of the jin technique is to show your bonsai's age as well as its ability to survive the struggle over time. For this technique, you would have to completely remove the bark of the branch from a certain starting point. After doing this, the remaining wood starts to die, and this forms the jin.

Creating a jin at the top of your bonsai gives you a result that's highly visible. The reason for this is that the tapered bonsai goes through a proportion change that has a significant effect on the illusion of age. This technique allows you to remove branches that you don't want to be part of your bonsai. This helps increase the age illusion as it creates a shape that is bent over. The illusion you create will look like a branch near your bonsai's trunk that has been broken.

- Sabamiki

The term "sabamiki" means split or hollowed trunk. For this technique, it would make your bonsai look like lightning has struck its surface. It would also make your bonsai look like its trunk has been damaged badly causing it to wither away. The technique involves stripping the bark from your bonsai's trunk. Then you would carve and drill the trunk to create a deep wound and expose its wood. However, you must make sure that the wound you create doesn't affect the nutrient flow of your bonsai to prevent it from dying. To do this, you need to apply a special type of preservative after performing the technique.

- Takuni

This is one of the more interesting techniques as you would use a piece of deadwood to for creating a composite style of driftwood. This technique gives your bonsai a weathered appearance. With it, you can also use the lower part of your bonsai. For this, you would carve a channel or a groove into the trunk then place living material. Young juniper trees are ideal for this technique because they are flexible and they're able to withstand severe shaping. For this technique, you would make use of wire wrappings, screws, and even nails. Once these are placed firmly, you can continue cultivating the tree.

- Uro

You can apply this technique to broadleaf types of bonsai. These types of bonsai typically have dead branches that fall off after they rot. When this happens, it creates a tiny hollow from the branch's indentation. After some time, this develops into a wound with an irregular shape on the trunk—this is the uro. Removing a branch from your bonsai to form a uro helps prevent scarring.

CHAPTER 10

INDOOR AND OUTDOOR BONSAI

Bonsai trees can be grown both indoors and outdoors. In fact, this is an important factor to consider when you're choosing the type of bonsai to grow. There are certain types which only thrive indoors—where the temperatures remain constant—and there are certain types which thrive better when placed outside. Deciding whether to place your bonsai indoors or outdoors can be quite a challenge as you need to consider a number of factors.

If you decide to place your bonsai indoors, the best location would be in the southern part of your home next to a window. This is because most types of bonsai require a lot of sunlight to remain healthy. Placing a bonsai tree away from sunlight will slow down its growth until it finally withers and dies. Most indoor bonsai trees are those belonging to tropical and sub-tropical varieties which require a relatively high level of humidity. Also, these trees should be placed somewhere with a temperature that doesn't change.

If you decide to place your bonsai outdoors, you should monitor it regularly. Since your bonsai will be exposed to the elements, it's important to keep checking it for pests, signs of disease, withering, and more. Also, you should consider the weather and seasonal changes for outdoor bonsai. Doing this ensures that your bonsai will grow and develop well while remaining healthy and strong.

Differences Between Indoor and Outdoor Bonsai

Deciding to become a bonsai grower will be both challenging and rewarding for you. Bonsai trees are beautiful, serene, and rewarding to grow. You can grow your bonsai indoors or outdoors depending on a number of factors. Here are some facts about indoor and outdoor bonsai to illustrate their differences:

- Indoor Bonsai

BONSAI

- These trees typically originate from the tropics thus, they survive well when grown in a similar climate.

- Some examples of indoor bonsai trees that are suitable for beginners include sago palms, bougainvillea, schefflera, gardenias, and a few elm types.

- Most indoor plants shed their leaves during the winter months, making them more vulnerable.

- They need to be exposed to the morning and afternoon sunlight.

- You can treat indoor bonsai the same way as other house plants apart from the special techniques used for bonsai growing.

- You can also use incandescent or fluorescent lights for indoor bonsai on cloudy, gloomy or rainy days.

- Pinching and pruning indoor bonsai are essential for you to help it reach the shape you desire. It's recommended to do these during spring to give you better control over your plant's growth.

- Outdoor Bonsai

- These trees are able to withstand different temperatures, even the freezing cold temperatures of the winter season.

- Outdoor bonsais are significantly bigger than those grown indoors. Also, they are stronger because they're able to survive in different kinds of weather conditions.

- There are two types of outdoor bonsai—deciduous trees and evergreens.

- Outdoor bonsai won't survive when grown indoors for long periods of time. However, you shouldn't leave them out in the freezing cold throughout the winter season either.

- For outdoor bonsai trees, you need to water them correctly and monitor them carefully. Do this to ensure that your outdoor bonsai is growing, developing, and is still healthy.

- It's more important to check the moisture of the soil for outdoor bonsai regularly. This helps you determine whether you need to water your plant or not. You must never allow the soil of an outdoor bonsai to dry up as this might kill the plant.

- Although fertilizing outdoor bonsais is important, you shouldn't fertilize your outdoor bonsai during winter as this is the dormant period.

For you to choose the right bonsai for yourself, you must determine whether you can grow it outdoors or indoors. Now that you know the characteristics of and differences between these bonsai classifications, you can make a better decision on which bonsai to grow.

Growing Indoor Bonsai

If you decide to grow a tropical or subtropical type of bonsai tree, then you should grow it indoors where you can maintain a stable temperature for it all through the year. There are many types of bonsais that can grow indoors such as Ficus, Hade, Sweet Plum, Hawaiian Umbrella, and more. Although caring for an indoor bonsai is a lot like caring for other house plants, there are certain differences since bonsai trees are special and unique kinds of plants. Here are some tips for you when growing indoor bonsai:

- Indoor bonsai training

Training an indoor bonsai isn't that different from training an outdoor bonsai. Therefore, all the tips and techniques we have already discussed apply to your indoor bonsai as well.

- Level of humidity

Indoor bonsai trees require a relatively high level of humidity—usually, they require a level that's higher than the one in your home. To increase humidity, you can place your bonsai on a humidity tray. Also, you can mist your bonsai throughout the day. If you can open one of the windows in the room where your bonsai is placed. That could help out too.

- Light

When it comes to light, the main issue with indoor

bonsai is that it won't get as much light as an outdoor plant. Although your bonsai won't die when it doesn't receive a lot of light, the rate of growth may decrease. This, in turn, will weaken your tree. This is why it's important to think about the placement of your bonsai—it's best to place it by a window where sunlight can shine upon it. If you think that your bonsai still isn't getting all the light it needs, you can use grow lights as a supplement.

- Pinching and trimming

These techniques help maintain the small size of your bonsai. Remember, indoor bonsai are significantly smaller in size compared to outdoor bonsai. It's important to trim and pinch the new growths far from the safe point. Also, you shouldn't remove all of the new growths. Make sure to leave some to maintain your tree's health. Various tropical and sub-tropical trees have various growth rates as well. Therefore, you must assess your own bonsai's growth rate and only perform pinching and trimming as needed.

- Placement of your bonsai

Even though you're growing an indoor bonsai, you can also place it outside once in a while—especially during spring, summer, and early autumn when the climate is warm. When placing your bonsai outdoors, make sure it gets a lot of sunlight, especially in the morning and in the afternoon. But during the late autumn and winter seasons, it's best to keep your bonsai indoors all day, every day. The reason for this is that indoor bonsais aren't able to thrive in cold weather. So when these seasons come along, it's time to confine your bonsai inside your home until the next spring .

- Preventing diseases and insect infestations

Even if your bonsai is a smaller version of a regular tree and you're growing it indoors, it's still susceptible to diseases and insect infestations. This is another thing you must watch out for when observing and evaluating your bonsai. If you think that your bonsai is suffering from a disease or if you discover that it's infested with pests, it's time to take some action. You need to treat your plant immediately, so the condition doesn't worsen.

- Repotting your bonsai

You must re-pot your indoor bonsai regularly—as soon as its root system has completely filled the container. Repotting allows you to provide your bonsai with fresh, new soil. It also encourages your plant to survive on a smaller root system. Generally, deciduous trees need to be repotted every two years or so, while evergreens may be repotted every four years. Again, different types of trees have different growth rates, so you must assess your own bonsai first. This helps you determine when you need to repot your plant.

- Temperature of the environment

Indoor bonsais require a constant temperature that's relatively high. Therefore, you must ensure that the room you place your bonsai in has this temperature to ensure that it grows and develops well.

- Watering your bonsai

For indoor plants, watering routinely isn't recommended. Instead, it's better to observe your tree and check the moisture level of the soil. Only water your indoor bonsai as needed.

Growing Outdoor Bonsai

One of the most common misconceptions about bonsais is that you should only grow them indoors. But the fact is, there are more types of bonsai trees that would survive and thrive better when grown outside. These bonsai trees need to be exposed to the seasons with changes in temperature, and the humidity level that's relatively high. Taking care for an outdoor bonsai differs from how you would take care of indoor plants. If you have chosen to care for an outdoor bonsai, here are some tips to help you out:

- Level of humidity

Even if your tree is growing outdoors, this doesn't mean that it's getting the proper level of humidity it needs to thrive. If you think the humidity in your area isn't high enough, you may place your bonsai on a humidity tray the same way you would with an indoor bonsai.

- Light

Most types of outdoor bonsais require sunlight exposure at least a couple of hours each day. Otherwise, their leaves and internodes will end up growing too big which, in turn, places them at an increased risk of developing diseases and insect infestations. The exception to this rule is coniferous trees which require full sunlight to grow healthy and strong.

- Outdoor bonsai training

Training an outdoor bonsai isn't that different from training an indoor bonsai. Therefore, all the tips and techniques we have already discussed apply to your outdoor bonsai as well.

- Pinching and trimming

These techniques help maintain the small size of your bonsai. Outdoor bonsai are significantly bigger in size compared to indoor bonsai. It's important to trim and pinch the new growths far from the safe point but you shouldn't remove all of the new growths. Leave some to maintain the health of your tree. Different outdoor trees have different growth rates too. Therefore, you must assess your bonsai's growth rate and only perform pinching and trimming as needed.

- Placement of your bonsai

Outdoor bonsais are living trees with a smaller size. They are not considered house houseplants, so you shouldn't treat them as such. During winter, there are some cases when you don't have to bring your bonsai indoors. Instead, you can just prepare your bonsai to help it survive the cold season. There are a few ways to do this:

  - First, you can bury your bonsai in the groups without its container. Choose a place that will keep your tree protected from the sun and wind, but not from the snow or rain.

  - You can also place your bonsai in a shed or in a garage without heating. Since your bonsai will enter a dormant state during this season, you don't have to expose it to sunlight. However, you must water it as needed.

For the other seasons, you can keep your bonsai outside—in a place where it can get a lot of sunlight. It's okay to bring your bonsai indoors once in a while, like if you want to display it on special occasions. However, you shouldn't keep it indoors for a long time as the constant temperature inside your home isn't healthy for an outdoor bonsai.

- Preventing diseases and insect infestations

Outdoor bonsai are much more prone to diseases and insect infestations because they are exposed to the elements. Therefore, you must check your tree regularly to ensure that it doesn't suffer from these conditions. As soon as you discover that your tree has a disease or that pests are starting to infest your tree, take steps immediately to remedy the situation.

- Repotting your bonsai

Repotting outdoor bonsai is essential as well. The best time to repot your tree is during the middle of the summer season. To do this, remove your bonsai—along with its old soil—from the container. Then remove the bottom and outer parts of your bonsai's root mass. Rake the soil away first, then start pruning the roots—just make sure that you don't prune too much as this might hinder the growth of your plant after repotting. After repotting, make sure to water your plant thoroughly to help it recover.

- Temperature of the environment

Outdoor bonsais are able to endure different temperatures. They don't require a constant high temperature as indoor bonsais do. In fact, they're designed to withstand the changing seasons. However, when winter comes along, you may want to bring your bonsai indoors, especially when you think the temperature outside is too cold for your plant to survive.

- Watering your bonsai

Watering outdoor bonsai is a bigger challenge compared to watering indoor bonsai. For instance, on hot and humid days, you may have to water your tree more frequently. The point is, since your tree is growing in the great outdoors, you need to monitor its soil regularly to check whether it's time to water or not. If you allow your bonsai to remain outdoors even when it's raining, this means that you can skip the watering session. Just keep checking the soil's moisture to be sure.

CHAPTER 11

BONSAI SEASONAL CARE TIPS

Whether you plan to grow an indoor bonsai or an outdoor one, it's important to learn how to care for your tree throughout the year, even as the seasons change. This is especially true since there are certain things you must do—and those you must avoid—during certain seasons. Knowing these things makes you more efficient at growing and caring for your miniature tree.

Interventions done throughout the life of your bonsai must have a purpose. If you want to have the mature bonsai tree that you had pictured in your mind, then it's best to interfere as little as possible with the natural activity of your bonsai. Also, you should know exactly when these interventions must be done in order to get the best results. For this, it's important to know that bonsai trees undergo a certain cycle each year wherein they go through different phases including:

- **Dormancy during the winter season:** This occurs because of very cold or freezing temperatures.

- Revival, emergence, and flowering during spring: This occurs during the early part of the season.

- Producing fruit and new growth during spring: This occurs throughout the season.

- Dormancy during the summer season (this period of dormancy is shorter): This occurs because of extremely high temperatures.

- Consolidation of new growth by the end of the summer season: The growth of the tree also stabilizes during this time.

- **Preparation for winter dormancy during autumn:** The tree starts preparing to go into the dormant state once again.

The points when these phases begin and how long they last depend on any changes in what's known as the "photoperiod"—the relationship between how long daytime lasts and how long nighttime lasts. The climate can also play a role in these phases as it can change the periods of activity or dormancy.

Whenever you want to intervene with the growth of your plant, you would have to do this during appropriate times or seasons throughout the life cycle of your tree. There are cases where you have the luxury of time—like if you can do a certain activity throughout an entire season—but there are also cases when you only have a matter of days or a few weeks to complete an activity—otherwise, you would have to wait for the next season to come along. There are general guidelines for you to follow, but you should also do your own research in order to learn more specific recommendations for your own geographical position.

Caring for Your Bonsai During Spring

Although spring is the season for revival and growth, it's also one of the most dangerous seasons for bonsais—especially if you don't practice patience. Throughout winter, your bonsai has been able to rest and it's now time to emerge and reward you with spectacular growth. However, if you don't care for your bonsai well during this season, you won't be able to witness this incredible sight.

If you are growing an outdoor bonsai, you would have moved it indoors to protect it from the freezing temperatures of winter. Come summer, leave your bonsai indoors for some time—this is where patience comes in—until you feel the warmth of summer.

Keep on checking your bonsai to determine whether you need to water it or not. On warm days, you may opt to open the windows of the shed or room you've placed your bonsai in. This helps your bonsai get some fresh air so that it won't get shocked when you move it outdoors once again. However, be sure to close the windows at night, especially if the nights are still very cold. When you notice that the temperature or the weather have stabilized—usually during the middle of the season—this is the time when you can place your bonsai back in the great outdoors.

If you are growing an indoor bonsai, you should have still taken good care of it throughout the winter season. During this time, your bonsai is vulnerable to conditions such as fungal infections, leaf drop, root rot, and more. As spring approaches, you shouldn't change what you have been doing to care for your bonsai during winter. However, there is one thing you must change.

While you had created a safe space for your bonsai to survive the cold winter inside your home, there is one thing that your plant would have been lacking: sunlight. This hunger for sunlight can manifest in a condition called leaf drop along with other symptoms like the soil being constantly wet and your bonsai having an overall unhealthy and yellowish appearance. To remedy this situation, make sure to expose your bonsai to natural sunlight on sunny days.

On gloomy days, place your plant under artificial lights, preferably fluorescent lights. Also, you have to reduce the frequency of watering your bonsai during winter and spring. As with outdoor bonsai, check the soil to determine whether it's time to water or not.

Caring for Your Bonsai During Summer

Summer is a volatile season for bonsais. How you would care for your tree depends on what type it is but generally, you should watch out for the temperature, humidity, and your plant's growth. For outdoor bonsais, you should have already placed your plant back outdoors by the end of spring. Even for indoor bonsai, you can place it outdoors once in a while as long as it's not too hot. And at night, don't forget to bring your indoor plant back inside your home.

For both indoor and outdoor bonsais, this season is when you should increase the frequency of watering, especially during the hottest days of summer. Check the moisture of your tree's soil frequently to make sure it doesn't dry out. For this season, here are the most important things to consider when it comes to watering your bonsai:

- It's a good practice to water your plant three times—one time for the plant, one time for the soil, and one time for the pot.

- You must water your bonsai regularly throughout the summer. Just one or two days of not watering the soil might end up killing the root ends of your bonsai. When this happens, it will affect the overall health of your tree.

- Misting the foliage of your bonsai isn't always enough, especially when you see that the soil has dried up.

Apart from watering your plant, it's also important to feed it with fertilizer. Combining water and fertilizer helps your bonsai remain healthy throughout the season. This season is also a time for rampant growth; therefore, you should do everything you can to promote this growth. Pruning is also an important thing to do during the summer. While spring is the best time to prune bonsai, you should still continue checking your tree for new growths that might turn it into a full-grown plant. Depending on the type of bonsai you're growing, you might have to prune and pinch every week.

The level of humidity is another issue during this season. Indoor bonsais are particularly at risk because it's usually more humid indoors than outdoors. When you're growing an outdoor bonsai and it's humid outside, you won't have to worry about this issue. But when the air inside your home is dry—especially when you use air-conditioning—the best thing to do is place your tree on a humidity tray with water. Also, avoid placing your bonsai in a drafty location as this might cause your plant to dry out.

Caring for Your Bonsai During Autumn

After summer comes autumn and this is the time when your bonsai is preparing for its winter dormancy. To help your tree prepare for the next season, you must make sure that it is at the peak of its health. Here are some pointers to help get your bonsai through autumn:

- Make sure your bonsai gets enough sun

During the summer, the sun is always overhead. But come autumn, it starts moving lower over the horizon. This may have an effect on the amount of sunlight your bonsai is exposed to depending on where you have placed it. The amount of sun your bonsai needs also depends on the type you're growing. There are some types which require more sunlight than others. If you know that your bonsai requires a lot of sun, you may have to move its location. On the other hand, if you're growing a deciduous tree, its leaves would already be falling off during this season, so you don't need to ensure that your plant is exposed to a lot of sunlight.

- Adjust your watering schedule

During this season, watering your bonsai can be quite tricky. If temperatures are starting to drop, you don't have to water your bonsai as frequently as you did during the summer. However, it's still important to check the soil regularly to make sure.

- Fertilize your bonsai regularly

Autumn is the season when you should be generous with feeding fertilizer. In fact, it's crucial for you to fertilize your bonsai during the autumn season. The reason for this is that the nutrients contained within the fertilizer will help prepare your bonsai for winter dormancy. Then as spring approaches, your bonsai will be strong enough to emerge and start its re-growth.

- Do the final pruning and wiring of your bonsai

It's never a good idea to prune or wire your bonsai during winter. Therefore, you should get these tasks out of the way before autumn ends. If you're growing a deciduous tree, you should do the final pruning as soon as it changes color. Make sure that you seal all of the cuts and wounds to help your tree recover and also to prevent the occurrence of sap loss.

- Other tips for autumn

BONSAI

- Make sure the surface of the soil is clean. To do this, sweep it clean and remove any coverings of weeds, moss, and even liverwort. This helps improve the circulation of air while preventing root rot.

- Use algae cleaner, deadwood preserver, and other types of bonsai products to keep your tree in tip-top shape.

- Make sure to check your plant, its container, and its environment to ensure that there are no pest infestations.

Caring for Your Bonsai During Winter

Winter is the season when bonsais go into a state of dormancy. Determining how to best care for your bonsai during this season depends on what type of tree you have and where you live. Outdoor bonsais are able to prepare and protect themselves from this season. But if the temperatures drop to freezing outside, you may consider bringing your bonsai indoors for a while. Of course, for indoor plants, they are already placed indoors. Just make sure that you place your bonsai in a room where you can maintain a constant warm temperature. Whether you have an outdoor or indoor bonsai, make sure that it's getting enough light and humidity throughout the season.

The most vulnerable part of bonsais during the winter season is the root system. When the temperatures are freezing, this part of the tree is highly susceptible to damage. Trees that grow in nature are buried deep in the ground; therefore, they don't get subjected to these freezing temperatures. Of course, this isn't the case for bonsais because they grow in small containers which are significantly shallow compared to trees in nature. This is why it's important to keep your bonsai warm during this season. Here are more tips to take care of your bonsai in winter:

- It's recommended to cover your tree with a newspaper wrap or a plastic over a piece of cloth. This will help promote heat during the cold season. As soon as the weather becomes warmer, you can remove these coverings to prevent the leaves from getting burned.

- It's also recommended to use grow lights during winter. Still, you should place your plant next to a window to allow for sunlight exposure each time the sun peeks out during the season.

- During winter, you should only water your bonsai when the soil dries out.

BONSAI

- If you choose not to bring your outdoor bonsai indoors during winter, you may want to cover the sides of its container with bubble wrap. This will keep your bonsai protected from the cold.

- Another option if you don't want to bring your bonsai indoors is to plant it in your garden during the winter season. This will help protect the roots of your bonsai. Then when spring comes, you can dig your bonsai out from the ground and place it in a pot.

- Continue checking your bonsai for signs of infestation so you can treat it right away as needed.

After winter, spring comes once again. Then you can apply the tips and strategies we had discussed for this season. This is a never-ending cycle and the longer you care for your bonsai, the more comfortable you will be in terms of growing and cultivating it. And the more experience you gain, the better and more efficient you will become at caring for your bonsai.

CHAPTER 12

MISTAKES TO AVOID WHEN GROWING BONSAI TREES

You must be very careful when growing bonsai. This process is a long-term commitment that requires patience, attention to detail, and a working knowledge of the different skills needed for cultivation, care, shaping, and styling your tree. While most people would feel tempted to "move the process along," your patience will come into play as it is more recommended to just allow your plant to "do its thing."

This is especially true at the beginning since all young bonsais have to do is grow. You don't have to shape and style your bonsai while still young, all you have to do is wait for it to reach the appropriate stage so you can start working on the aesthetics. While waiting, make sure to check your young bonsai frequently to ensure that it's growing and developing well. When it comes to growing bonsai, there are several mistakes you should avoid. These mistakes are very common, especially among beginners and they can have a detrimental effect on the growth of your tree. It's useful to learn these mistakes so that you can avoid them as much as possible.

Be Aware of and Avoid These Common Mistakes

Making a commitment to grow a bonsai is a huge task. It requires a lot of careful thought and you should open yourself to the possibility of encountering issues along the way. Growing bonsai is challenging and rewarding at the same time. To help you become an effective beginner bonsai grower, try to avoid these common mistakes:

1. Choosing the wrong type of tree

Although you may have your heart set on growing a particular type of tree, you should do research about it first. This will help you determine whether you can grow that type of tree successfully or not. Otherwise, you would end up with a bonsai that was doomed from the very start. Remember the different factors to consider when choosing a tree. Keep those factors in mind so you can make the right choice.

2. Not being familiar with the tree you've

chosen to grow

When you've decided on the tree you want to grow, then you should learn all that you can about it. The more familiar you are with the tree you've chosen, the better you will be at growing it. Conversely, if you try growing a tree that you know nothing about, you might do things that are detrimental to the health of that tree.

3. Planting your bonsai in an inappropriate environment

This is one of the reasons why it's important to learn as much as you can about the tree you plan to grow. For instance, trying to grow a bonsai that's meant to grow indoors in your garden won't be a successful endeavor. You should make sure that the environment you plant your bonsai in is just right to ensure that it grows into a strong and healthy miniature tree.

4. Pruning your tree too much or too frequently

Although pruning is an important process for the health and appearance of your bonsai, you shouldn't go overboard. Pruning properly promotes the growth of your bonsai while shaping it according to your plans. However, over-pruning your bonsai can negatively affect its ability to make nutrients and absorb sunlight. Also, make sure to use the proper tools when pruning your bonsai so you don't damage it.

5. Performing several techniques simultaneously

There are different techniques involved in growing, shaping, and styling bonsai. But you should never perform all of these techniques at the same time. This will cause too much stress to your bonsai. For instance, after repotting or wiring your bonsai, give it some time to recover. Think of it this way: the process of pruning your bonsai is a lot like a person having surgery. After performing the procedure, you should give your bonsai enough time to heal before you perform another technique such as wiring or pinching.

CONCLUSION

PLANTING YOUR OWN BONSAI

By now you have all the basic information you need to start growing your own bonsai. We had gone through all of the bonsai fundamentals to arm you with the knowledge you need to choose a bonsai, plant it, cultivate it, and help it grow and mature to the bonsai of your dreams. Bonsais are truly an art form from their history, their symbolism, how they are grown and cultivated, and how they look when they reach maturity. Whether you're an art lover or you just want to have your own bonsai in your home, your journey will always start with planting.

The great thing about bonsais is that there are different types available. Basically, any tree you see in nature can be grown as a bonsai. So if you have a favorite type of tree, you may start doing research about it specifically to help you determine if you can successfully grow that type of tree in your area. The

BONSAI

key to being able to grow bonsai is to learn as much as you can about the process. In this book, we had gone through all the general information you need. Once you have chosen the type of bonsai to grow, then you can start learning more about it.

Although growing bonsai is a challenging task which requires a lot of patience, the reward you would get from being able to grow one into maturity will be worth it. From the time you decide to start growing a bonsai to the time you're actually growing it, you would have a lot of things to do and consider. Also, keep in mind that this is a lifelong process because bonsais have very long lifespans. With all this information at your disposal, all you have to do now is find the bonsai of your dreams and start growing!

BONSAI

Made in the USA
San Bernardino,
CA